D1106534

S.RUDE '05

Mike Baron • Steve Rude

Nexus

Volume Three

NEXUS **CREATED BY**

Mike Baron

and Steve Rude

FOREWORD BY

Ron Marz

DARK HORSE BOOKS™

PUBLISHER
Mike Richardson

COLLECTION DESIGNER
Heidi Fainza

COLLECTION EDITOR
Dave Land

ART DIRECTOR
Lia Ribacchi

Published by
Dark Horse Books
A division of Dark Horse Comics, Inc.

Dark Horse Comics, Inc.
10956 SE Main Street
Milwaukie, Oregon 97222

darkhorse.com
bloodyredbaron.com
steverude.com

To find a comic shop in your area, call the
Comic Shop Locator Service: (888) 266-4226

First Edition: May 2006
ISBN: 1-59307-495-6

1 3 5 7 9 10 8 6 4 2

Printed in China

NEXUS™ ARCHIVES: VOLUME THREE

This volume collects issues twelve through eighteen of *Nexus* Volume Two originally published by First Comics.

TABLE OF CONTENTS

WRITTEN BY MIKE BARON
ART BY STEVE RUDE

FOREWORD
by Ron Marz

I don't collect comics.

Yeah, I've got stacks of them in my office, stacks of them in the basement, a couple bookcases full of collected editions. But as far as actually collecting them—keeping obsessive checklists, trawling back-issue bins, tucking them away in mylar snuggies—I ain't interested. The musty aroma of *Eau de Old Comics* doesn't do a thing for me, except make me want to sneeze. To me, the most valuable comics are the dog-eared ones that have been well read and well loved.

But I do have a box that contains the complete run on *Nexus*. Every single issue. In order. Even the black-and-white ones.

I came of age, comics-wise, in the 1980s, when the appearance of *Dark Knight Returns* and *Watchmen* spawned an endless series of newspaper articles inevitably titled "Bam! Pow! Zap! Comics Aren't Just for Kids Anymore!" Those books are touchstones for everybody who was reading comics in that era. They opened my mind to the possibilities of comics being more than the DC and Marvel slugfests I read (and enjoyed) as a kid. They also opened my mind to looking beyond Marvel and DC, to other companies, other comics, among them Matt Wagner's *Grendel*, Ostrander and Truman's *Grimjack*, Chaykin's *American Flagg!*, and of course Baron and Rude's *Nexus*.

I'm not sure which issue was my first. But I'm sure it was a First. I didn't make my initial trip to Ylum until *Nexus* had landed at First Comics after starting life at Capital. I'd like to say my first exposure to *Nexus* was one of the issues in this volume. And it may well have been. But the truth is, I just don't remember, and it really doesn't matter anyway. Whatever issue was my first, I was enthralled by it. I trawled back-issue bins to find out what I'd missed.

I discovered a story that didn't rely on superhero tropes. The hero (could you even call him a hero?) killed people. People who deserved it, but *still*. Horatio Hellpop was as tortured and compelling a protagonist as there's been in comics, surrounded by a rich cast including Dave and Judah the Thunes, the Heads, duplicitous Ursula, and the lovely Sundra. Come on, who didn't fall in love with Sundra, at least a little?

All this from a couple of guys who got their start in that Mecca of sequential inspiration, Wisconsin.

Mike Baron's credits list is as long as my arm, but *Nexus* is his masterwork, infused with his manic passion. No other series has ever slipped back and forth so effortlessly between action, pathos, and sheer lunacy. Baron covered all the bases, and was equally adept at all of them: comedy and tragedy, sex and violence, politics and social commentary. Other comics from the Big Two took place in a shared "universe." But *Nexus* didn't need one. It was a universe unto itself, with a fully realized history and political structure.

The other half of the equation was the Dude, the yin to Baron's yang, bringing everything to life in bold lines like the glorious bastard child of Kirby,

Toth, Rockwell, and Loomis. Steve Rude's work is perhaps the purest synthesis of classic comics tradition and classic American illustration. The Dude is still one of my favorites, still at the top of my "must work with someday" list.

And while we're at it, how 'bout Nexus' costume? If there's been a better costume design in comics the last quarter century, I haven't seen it. And neither have you.

On their own, Baron and Rude are good. Together, sparks fly. Together, there's *Nexus*. This book played a big part in helping me decide this was what I wanted to do, and in forming me as a writer. It's probably not a complete accident that space-faring material like *Silver Surfer* and *Green Lantern* form a decent chunk of my resumé. Thanks, Mike and Steve, for letting me stand on your shoulders.

In looking back at the issues contained in this volume, there's still a sense of *new* here—the same sense that permeated the series more than two decades ago. These stories aren't dated, the same way *Rubber Soul* sounds as contemporary now as it did in 1966. They're still new, still different.

Still better.

Vootie,
Ron Marz
cold, snowy upstate New York
January 2006

Ron Marz has written extensively for DC, Marvel, Image, and Dark Horse Comics, including his creator-owned series Samurai: Heaven and Earth. *He and his wife and their three children have returned to their native upstate New York after five years of dodging hurricanes in Florida.*

CHERNENKO--HUB OF THE DWINDLING SOV SYSTEM.

COMRADE ..?

NEXUS®

GENERAL KROGH? HORATIO HELLPOP OF THE FREE AND INDEPENDENT MOON YLUM. I UNDERSTAND YOU KNEW MY FATHER...

The Old General

Nothing is more seductive for man than his freedom of conscience. But nothing is a greater cause of suffering.

Fyodor Dostoyevsky

·Mike Baron·Steve Rude·Eric Shanower·Steve Haynie·Les Dorscheid·Rick Oliver·
·SCRIPT· ·PENCILS· ·INKS· ·LETTERS· ·COLORS· ·EDITS·

NO!! TED HELLPOP'S BOY? I CAN HARDLY BELIEVE IT! COME. SIT. WHAT BRINGS YOU TO CHERNENKO?
BUSINESS. I DEAL IN WHOLESALE WEIGHTS AND MEASURES.
OCK! DA! AND WE ARE FAMOUS FOR THE PRECISION OF OUR SCALES. BUT YOU WILL DINE WITH ME!

YES.

YOUR FATHER SERVED WITH ME ON EKKELET-- BEFORE HE WAS SENT TO VRADIC ...
HE TOLD ME MANY TIMES. HE SAID THAT IF I EVER NEEDED HELP WITHIN THE SOV SYSTEM, I SHOULD TALK TO THE OLD GENERAL.

OCK, DA! FOR THE SON OF TED HELLPOP, ANYTHING IN MY POWER.
TELL ME ABOUT MY FATHER ...
STOLICH
IMPORTED FR
Stolich
vodka
RUSSIAN V

AND SO, LONG INTO THE NIGHT...
OCK, HE WAS BRAVE AND TRUE, AND FILLED WITH THE IDEALIST'S PASSION. AS WE ALL WERE IN THOSE DAYS... THOSE BRIGHT AND SHINING DAYS OF OUR YOUTH...
GENERAL ...
THEODORE HELLPOP

HOW HAVE YOU REMAINED ALIVE FOR SIX HUNDRED YEARS?

YOU KNOW --?
3

YOU DON'T EXACTLY HIDE THE FACT. WHO IS THIS STANDING NEXT TO KHRUSCHEV AT THE 1960 MAY DAY PARADE IN RED SQUARE ON EARTH?
AND AT THE OLYMPIC CEREMONIES ON POTEMKIN, ZIZO? YOU'VE MASTERED IMMORTALITY, HAVEN'T YOU?
IT IS THE MOST CLOSELY GUARDED SECRET IN THE SOV SYSTEM. BUT I WILL TELL TED HELLPOP'S BOY.
CELLS ARE SAVED FOR CLONING. WHEN THE OLD BODY IS NEAR COLLAPSE, THE NEW ONE IS PREPARED AT A ROUGH CHRONOLOGICAL AGE OF NINE.
THE CLONE, OF COURSE, HAS NO TIME TO DEVELOP A PERSONALITY. THE TRANSFERRAL IS A COMBINATION OF COMPLEX NEURAL ATTACHMENTS AND ANCIENT EASTERN MEDITATION TECHNIQUES...
WHY DO YOU RISK DISCOVERY, THEN, BY RETURNING AS YOURSELF?
FAR EASIER TO REINTRODUCE ONESELF AS A CHILD. NATURALLY, WE HAVE CAREFULLY PREPARED OUR COVER IDENTITY...
4

THE TRUTH, THEN, IS THAT I AM HERE TO EXECUTE YOU FOR YOUR CRIMES.

I HAVE HEARD OF YOU ...SO YOU ARE ***NEXUS***...

THE TRUTH, NOW, GENERAL. DIDN'T YOU SUSPECT I MIGHT SOMEDAY COME?

WE LINED THEM UP AND WE SHOT THEM. THAT IS HOW WE DEALT WITH THE STATE'S ENEMIES. YOUR FATHER DID THE SAME.
MY FATHER HAS PAID FOR HIS CRIMES.
NOW THAT YOU ARE HERE, IT SEEMS LIKE THE MOST NATURAL THING IN THE WORLD...

MAY I LOOK IN ON MY GRANDSON?
CERTAINLY.
M.P.

MIDDLE
REGISTRA
name
Miroslav Pa

LENIN
MIDDL
REGISTRAT
name
Miroslav Papel

LENIN MI
MIDDLE
REGISTRATIO

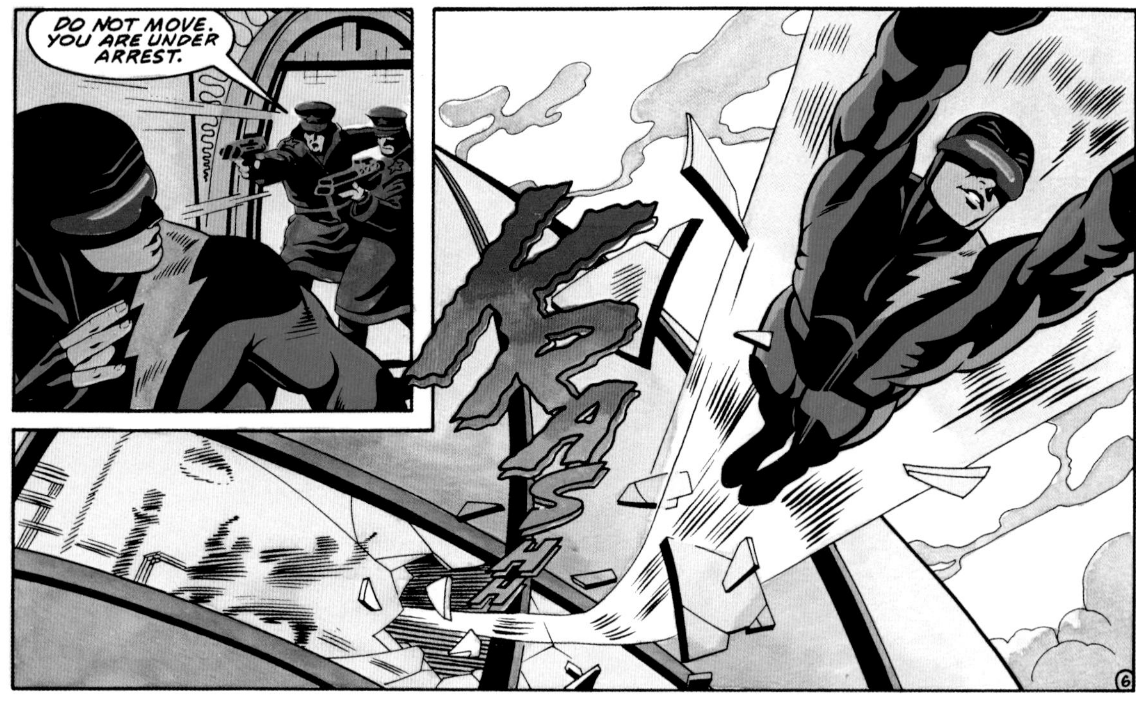
DO NOT MOVE. YOU ARE UNDER ARREST.
KRASHH
6

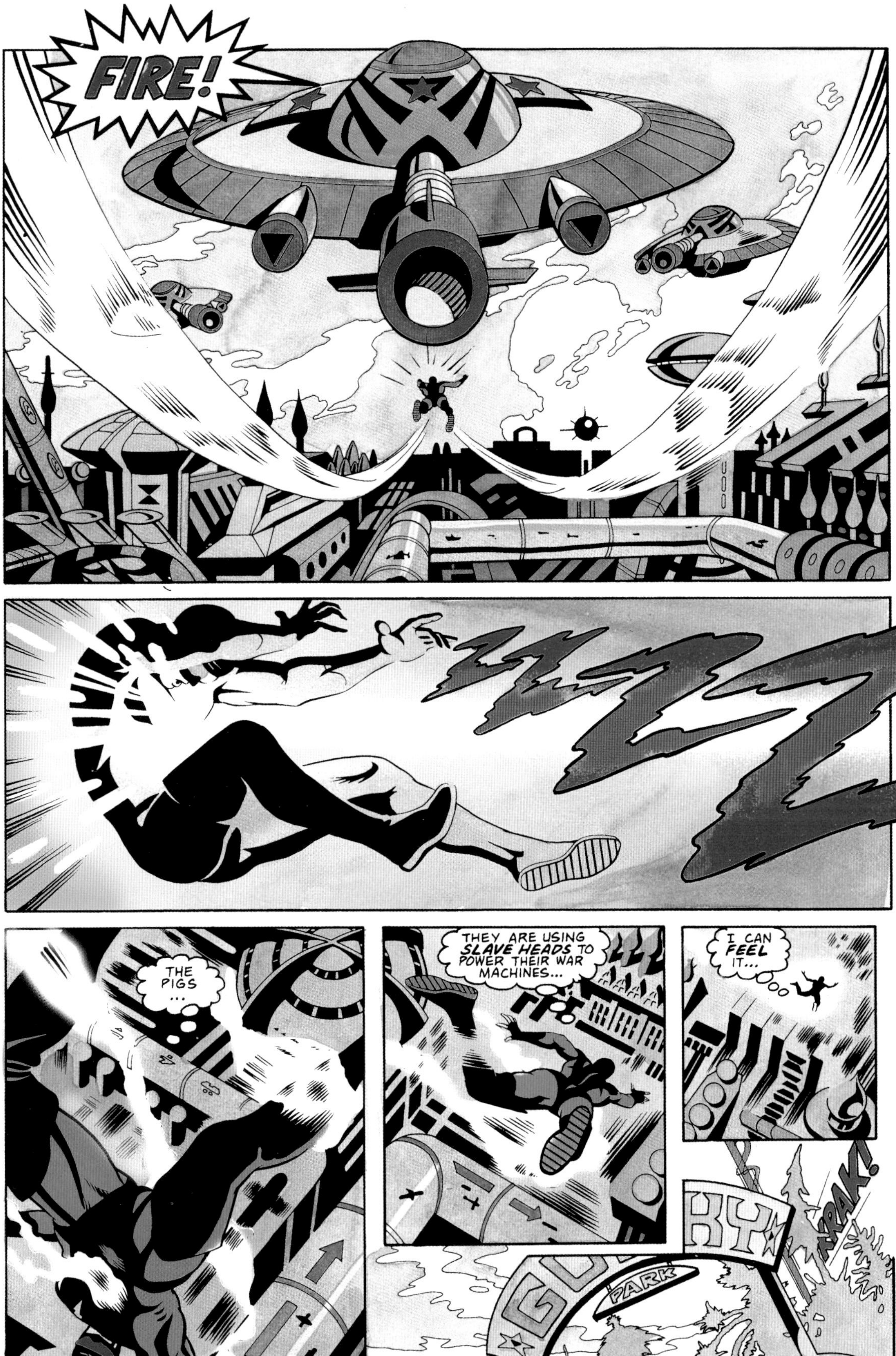

FIRE!

THE PIGS ...
THEY ARE USING **SLAVE HEADS** TO POWER THEIR WAR MACHINES...
I CAN **FEEL** IT...
PARK
KRAK!
7

IT'S HAPPENING TOO FAST. I NEED TIME.
BUT I CAN'T WALK AROUND LIKE THIS...

I COULD MAKE MYSELF CLOTHES OUT OF RANDOM MATTER... BUT IT WOULDN'T LOOK QUITE RIGHT...
ZZZZAP!

HMM...

MOMENTARILY.
COMRADE, EXCUSE ME...
SHUTTLE
DA? GO ON --BEAT IT OR I REPORT YOU, YOU DRUNK.

I AM NOT A DERELICT.
WHO BUT A DERELICT WOULD CAVORT THROUGH GURKY PARK IN SUB-ZERO WEATHER? AND IN TIGHTS YET!

I AM A DANCER WITH THE CHERNENKO BALLET! AND I AM IN THE PARK BECAUSE I AM RESEARCHING THE PART OF DR. ZHIVAGO! YOU BESMIRCH THE PEOPLE'S ART WITH YOUR VULGAR ASSUMPTIONS...

I SHOULD REPORT YOU!
GULP
8

BUT COMRADE, I MEANT NO HARM! A SIMPLE JEST...
HMM... NOW THAT YOU MENTION IT, IT IS A BIT BRISK OUT HERE. THE PEOPLE'S BALLET DIRECTOR WILL BE FURIOUS IF I SHOULD CATCH A CHILL... HE WILL ASK WHAT HAS DELAYED ME...

PLEASE-- TAKE MY COAT. I INSIST!
THANKS, COMRADE.
WHAT DID YOU WANT TO ASK ME ABOUT?
WHAT? OH... DO YOU HAVE THE TIME?

6:15. LOOK-- DO YOU WANT MY WATCH? THE HAT?
SHUTTLE
NO THANK YOU. YOU'VE BEEN MORE THAN KIND.

SOON.
COMRADE, EXCUSE ME...
DA?

DO YOU KNOW WHAT THIS IS? I FOUND IT IN THE PARK.
AGNEW

GASP! A GENUINE WEB ARTIFACT! IT'S WORTH... HUNDREDS! I GIVE YOU 200 RUPLES FOR IT!
$\frac{Я200 \times 9.15 \div K}{S^2}$ = 1900
500.

300
400
350

EUREKA!
SHUTTLE
GURKY
PARK
I COULD EASILY HAVE DUPLICATED THIS SPECIE, BUT WHO AM I TO COUNTERFEIT THE OVERBURDENED RUPLE?
HATED TO GIVE UP THE PINBACK--I'M SURE THE BADGER WOULD UNDERSTAND.
9

HATS

STUFFED MUTANT SALMON?
I'LL TAKE TWO.

COMRADE-- SHOW US YOUR PAPERS.
I DON'T HAVE ANY PAPERS.
COME WITH US PLEASE.

I AM NEXUS.
SURE YOU ARE. YOU'RE HEADED FOR A RE-EDUCATION CAMP, METHINKS.
IGOR, WHAT DID YOU FIND?

SOME KIND OF DISGUISE.
10

SHORTLY, IN A DESERTED WAREHOUSE.
WHAT HAVE WE GOT HERE?
TELL ME, COMRADES --ARE YOU HAPPY?
WE'LL ASK THE QUESTIONS.
NAME?

NOW I HAVE PAPERS ...
AUSE
HOURS
7-9PM
UT PROPER AUTHORIZATION

THE SOVS WOULD LEVEL THE BLOCK TO GET AT ME.
GASTRONOM

HOW CAN I GET BACK INTO THE GENERAL'S APARTMENT WITHOUT ENDANGERING EVERYONE IN THE BUILDING?
I CAN'T.

HOW THEN IF I WALK AWAY? I CAN'T LET THE INNOCENT DIE TO PUNISH THE GUILTY.
TUBE WAY

TUBE WAY

TUBE WAY

TUBE WAY
FOOSH

I... GET...THE... PICTURE...
TUBE WAY

THIS CALLS FOR HYPER-SPEED.

YURI, I'M GETTING AN INTENSE ENERGY FLUCTUATION.
ALERT CENTRAL AND STAND BY-- THIS COULD BE IT!
VAM!
GASTRONOM
TRANYA

HELLPOP, DO YOUR DUTY!

HELLPOP, DO YOUR DUTY!
12

INFORM CENTRAL THAT THE ALIEN AGENT HAS BEEN **TERMINATED.**

GROUND LEVEL-- 1.5 KILOMETERS BELOW.
CALL THE MILITIA! TELL THEM WE NEED **MORE AMBULANCES!**
ARE YOU ALL RIGHT, BUBUSHKA?
YES, THANK YOU. BUT WHAT HAPPENED?
I DON'T KNOW. I WISH I COULD STAY AND HELP THE WOUNDED.
13

STATE SECURITY.
YES COMRADE. HOW CAN I HELP YOU?

LENIN MIDDL
SCHOOL
DO YOU HAVE A STUDENT NAMED MIROSLAV PAPELOVICH STRANSKY?
LET ME CHECK OUR COMLINK...
STRANSKY IS IN STATE HISTORY, ROOM 603.

ZZK
CLASS, TODAY WE ARE GOING TO LEARN ABOUT SOME OF THE GREAT **HEROES** OF THE SOV DYNASTY...

MEN AND WOMEN SUCH AS LENIN, EMMA GOLDMAN, AND GENERAL KROGH...
COMRADE TEACHER ...
ME

WHO ARE YOU?
I HAVE COME FOR MIROSLAV PAPELOVICH.

WHAT DO YOU MEAN, YOU'VE COME FOR HIM? BY **WHOSE** AUTHORITY?
I WISH I KNEW.
GRANDPA
ME

I'M NOT GOING TO HELP YOU.
NEVER MIND. I SEE HIM.

GENERAL KROGH --I HAVE COME FOR **YOU**.
NO! YOU'RE CRAZY! **HELP!**
COME WITH ME. I WON'T DO THIS HERE.
14

HURRY! A MANIAC IS SEIZING ONE OF MY STUDENTS!
I TRULY REGRET THIS INTRUSION.
HELP ME, SOMEBODY, PLEASE!

HELLPOP --WAIT!

I AM WHOM YOU SEEK.

COME WITH ME, GENERAL. I'M SORRY ABOUT UPSETTING YOUR GRANDSON.

YOU ARE NOT INFALLIBLE!
AND YOU ARE THE PEOPLE'S HERO...

TODAY.
15

ATTENTION NEXUS...
BZZZZZZZZZZGGG
LENIN MIDD
THE BUILDING IS COMPLETELY ENCLOSED IN A FORCE FIELD! YOU CANNOT ESCAPE! SURRENDER!
YOU HAVE TEN MINUTES! THEN WE WILL INTRODUCE ANTIMATTER INTO THE FIELD!

DON'T THEY KNOW WHO YOU ARE?
NO. ONLY THREE MEMBERS OF THE CENTRAL COMMITTEE--AND THEY NEED MY AUTHORITY TO INFORM STATE SECURITY.

BUT SURELY THE PRESENT SITUATION...
YES ...
LENI
IF THEY CAN BE REACHED IN THE NEXT TEN MINUTES.

WITH YOUR ARRIVAL I DECIDED TO TAKE A FRESH IDENTITY-- PREPARATIONS WERE MADE...
YOU LIED ABOUT THE TRANSFER, GENERAL. SOMETIMES YOU MUST DISPLACE A PERSONALITY.

TRUE.
FOOSH

16

HOLD YOUR FIRE!
I'M COMING OUT!

HERE I AM!

KILL ME... IF YOU CAN!

DEEP WITHIN THE KREMLIN,* IN CHERNENKO'S CAPITAL CITY.

COMRADES, TO THE MEMORY OF OUR BELOVED RUDY...

NOW THERE ARE THREE ...THREE **SURVIVORS** OF THE 20TH CENTURY.

THREE THAT WE **KNOW** OF...

* BY THE 26TH CENTURY, KREMLIN HAD BECOME THE GENERIC TERM FOR THE GOVERNING BUILDING ON EACH SOV PLANET. —R.A.O.

18

THE TECHNIQUE IS SECRET. EVEN NEXUS DIDN'T GET IT. BUT BY KILLING RUDY HE DID MORE THAN STRIKE AT THE CENTRAL COMMITTEE --HE OBLITERATED HISTORY!
WHAT DO YOU SUGGEST, BORIS?

HE DIES. WE FIND HIM, WE DESTROY HIM!
KONSTANTIN?

YES.

NATASHA?
DA.

THE PLANET MARLIS.
MOTHER... FATHER... I THINK ABOUT YOU OFTEN...

I HOPE YOU WOULD BE PROUD OF ME... I OFTEN DOUBT MYSELF...
BUT I DON'T SEEM TO HAVE ANY CHOICE IN THE MATTER. AND I'M GOOD AT IT.

FATHER, I MET A FRIEND OF YOURS RECENTLY ...

LET ME TELL YOU ABOUT IT...
19

YLUM.
ZOOM... ZOOM..!
WE'LL ISSUE A RECORD-- SUNDRA SINGS THE SOUNDS OF SPACE!
WOW-- NEAT!
eat at VOOPE

IN A REMOTE ROOM IN THE DESERTED "NEW WING..."
GREAT NEXUS, I CAME AT ONCE. I TOLD NO ONE. BUT WHY THISS SSECRECY? WHY NOT YOUR OWN QUARTERSS? NO ONE EVEN KNOWSS THAT YOU ARE BACK.
THIS MUST BE OUR LITTLE SECRET, XYP. I WANT THE IMPLANT. CAN WE BEGIN?
SANITIZE

FOR LONG HOURS, AIDED ONLY BY ROBOTS, XYP INSTALLS THE ELECTRODE THAT WILL ENABLE NEXUS TO CONTROL THE HEADACHES THAT DRIVE HIM TO THE TANK.

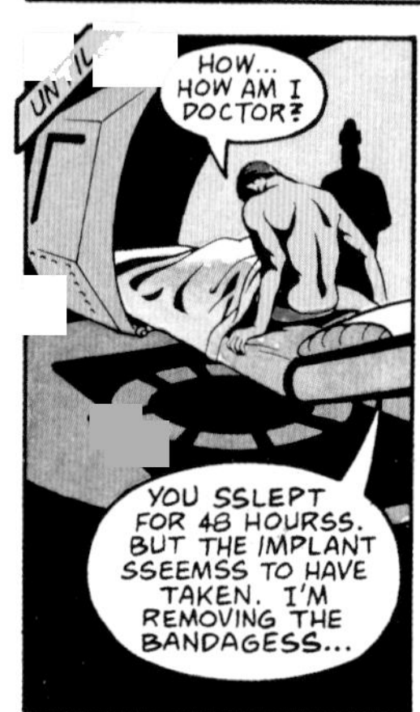
HOW... HOW AM I DOCTOR?
YOU SSLEPT FOR 48 HOURSS. BUT THE IMPLANT SSEEMSS TO HAVE TAKEN. I'M REMOVING THE BANDAGESS...

I FEEL GOOD.

I REALLY DO.
NEXT MONTH
INSOMNIA
20

A MARINE CAMP SERVING THE ***WEB***, AN INTERPLANETARY ORGANIZATION WITH HEADQUARTERS ON EARTH.

PEALE, YOU ARE THIS COMPANY'S OUTSTANDING CADET.

THANK YOU, COMMANDER IMADA.

DON'T THANK ME. AT EASE. YOUR INITIATIVE AND SURVIVAL SKILLS ARE EXTRAORDINARY. I'M FORMING A SPECIAL UNIT.

MIKE BARON
SCRIPT

ERIC SHANOWER
ART & LETTERS

LES DORSCHEID
COLORS

RICK OLIVER
EDITS

BENDING THE TWIG

THIS UNIT WILL BE FULLY AUTONOMOUS AND WILL ANSWER DIRECTLY TO ME. I WILL ANSWER DIRECTLY TO THE PRESIDENT. OUR PURPOSE WILL BE TO GATHER INTELLIGENCE. I WANT YOU TO JOIN.

CDR IMADA

THANK YOU, COMMANDER. THIS IS AN HONOR. DO I HAVE A CHOICE?

CHOICE? PEALE, DO YOU ***REALIZE*** WHAT THIS POSITION COULD DO FOR YOUR CAREER?

COME WITH ME.

SIR, I'M ON DUTY AT 21:30...

YOU HAVE BEEN ***RELIEVED*** OF ALL DUTY. YOU ARE OFFICIALLY ON LEAVE.

PEALE

OUR NEW UNIT, BRANCH CORPS, WILL BE VITAL TO WEB SECURITY.
HOW IS THAT, SIR?
THE WEB--A LOOSE AGGREGATION OF SOME 113 INHABITED WORLDS--IS BOUND TOGETHER OUT OF MUTUAL NEED. EARTH NEEDS TAU CETI'S MEDICINE. WOLF NEEDS EARTH'S TECHNOLOGY. AND EVERYBODY NEEDS ENERGY.
TCS

IT'S NO SECRET WE ARE STARVING FOR NEW FUELS. WHAT IS SECRET IS THAT THE ASTEROID MATTER CONVERSION PROJECT HAS FAILED. THE WEB MAY BE UNABLE TO SUPPLY ITSELF, LET ALONE MEET OBLIGATIONS TO CLIENTS.

BUT WE BELIEVE SEVERAL OF OUR CLOSEST TRADING PARTNERS ARE ENGAGED IN SECRET PROGRAMS.
ENERGY IS THE MOST VALUED COMMODITY. SO VALUABLE, OUR WEB ALLIES ARE CERTAINLY LYING WHEN THEY CLAIM THEY HAVE FOUND NO NEW SOURCES.
TCS
HANGAR

SIR, WHERE ARE WE GOING?
BRANCH CORPS WILL FIND OUT.

THIS IS THE HARD-SELL, PEALE. YOU'LL FIND A WARDROBE IN THE GUEST ROOM. WE'RE GOING OUT.
I WANT YOU TO HAVE A TASTE OF WHAT'S IN STORE.
2.

AHHHHHHHH..!
I'D FORGOTTEN HOW WONDERFUL A HOT BATH FEELS...

THEY KEPT REFERRING TO COMMANDER IMADA AS THE "DRAGON LADY." I THINK I SEE A GRAIN OF TRUTH.

WHAT TO WEAR, WHAT TO WEAR?

YOU LOOK FINE. TONIGHT, WE'LL JUST TALK. I WANT TO GET A SENSE OF YOUR PERSONAL GOALS, AND TO GIVE YOU AN IDEA HOW BRANCH CORPS WILL FIT IN.

AS A BRANCH OP, OR "TWIG," YOU'LL ADOPT A CIVILIAN IDENTITY. FULL EXPENSES AND A GENEROUS WAGE. PLEASE DO NOT BE COY, I KNOW THAT YOU ARE AMBITIOUS.

CRUSTACEAN CLUB
I, TOO, AM AMBITIOUS. IT IS A TRAIT I ADMIRE. I ***TRUST*** AMBITION.
3.

YOU'D BE JUST PERFECT FOR BRANCH CORPS. THIS WOULD BE YOUR MILIEU.
NO. YOU WOULD RECEIVE AN IMMEDIATE HONORABLE DISCHARGE. DO YOU GAMBLE?
DO I GET A **COMMISSION**?
I'VE PLAYED BACCARAT... HIGH STAKES RISK...
GOOD TO SEE YOU AGAIN, COMMANDER.

THAT'S FINE. AH. THIS IS OUR TABLE. MAY I ORDER FOR YOU?
PLEASE.

ARE YOU FAMILIAR WITH LIDDY?
NO...
20TH CENTURY PHILOSOPHER LIDDY. HE BELIEVED IN THE SUPREMACY OF THE **WILL**...

WILL HAS BROUGHT ME THIS FAR--IT WILL TAKE ME TO THE TOP. AND YOU, TOO.
WHAT IS THE TOP?

PRESIDENCY OF THE WEB, IF I WANT IT. OR PERHAPS SOMETHING I HAVEN'T EVEN **CONSIDERED**...

THAT IS UNIMPORTANT. WHAT **IS** IMPORTANT-- HOW I USE MY WILL. I AM GOING TO SHOW YOU SOMETHING, SUNDRA...
4

I WILL SHOW YOU SOMETHING I CAN TEACH YOU. THE CASINO IS FILLED WITH CONFIDENT, SELF-IMPORTANT MEN. CHOOSE ONE.
WHY?

I SWEAR, YOU ARE THE MOST CONTUMACIOUS MARINE I EVER MET! IT'S A MYSTERY HOW YOU MADE IT THROUGH BASIC TRAINING!

I HAVE THE ABILITY TO BEND A MAN TO MY WILL. CHOOSE. MAKE IT DIFFICULT.

HIM. THE LIZIGATOR.
NO ALIENS. SORRY. I SAID ANY MAN.

OKAY. THE BIG, BEEFY GUY IN THE BLUE TUX WITH THE SLIM BLOND WOMAN ON HIS ARM.

COME ON, BABIES, LOOK PRETTY FOR ME... ALL RIGHT!
MAY I PLAY HERE?
BY ALL MEANS, LITTLE LADY.
5.

FOLLOW MY LEAD, LITTLE LADY. YOU'LL MAKE SOME CREDIT.
THANK YOU. MAY I WHISPER SOMETHING TO YOU?
BY ALL MEANS, LITTLE LADY.

I WANT YOU TO GET DOWN ON YOUR HANDS AND KNEES AND CRAWL OUT OF THE CASINO.

WHAT?
YOU HEARD ME.

GET LOST, BIMBO.
WHY ON EARTH SHOULD I DO THAT?
TO HUMOR ME.

YOU'RE A WEIRDIE, LITTLE LADY. YOU KNOW THAT?
SO I'VE BEEN TOLD...

WHY DON'T YOU GET DOWN ON YOUR HANDS AND KNEES AND CRAWL OUT OF THE CASINO? HMM?
WHY... WHY... DON'T... WHY DON'T...
6.

HEY! WHAT ARE YOU DOING TO HIM? LEAVE HIM ALONE!

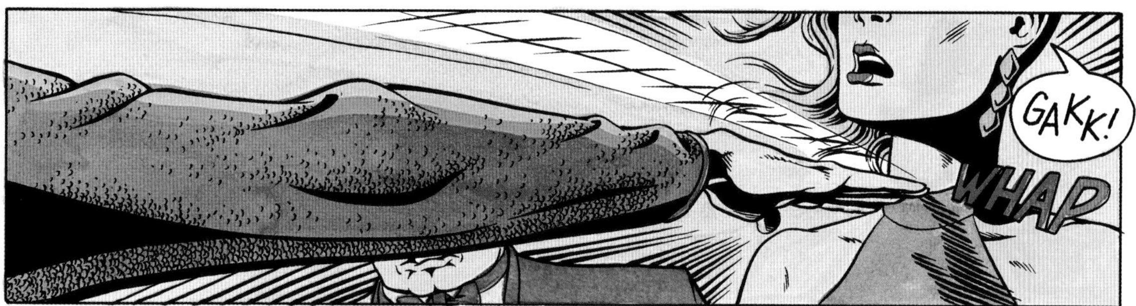
GAKK!
WHAP

ON YOUR HANDS AND KNEES...
MR. CRUIKSHANK, IT'S YOUR BET.
REX

MR. CRUIK-SHANK?

HA HA!
PLAYERS
7.

HOW DID YOU DO THAT?
SHALL WE?
SHE... (CHOKE!)... SHE DID SOMETHING TO HIM!

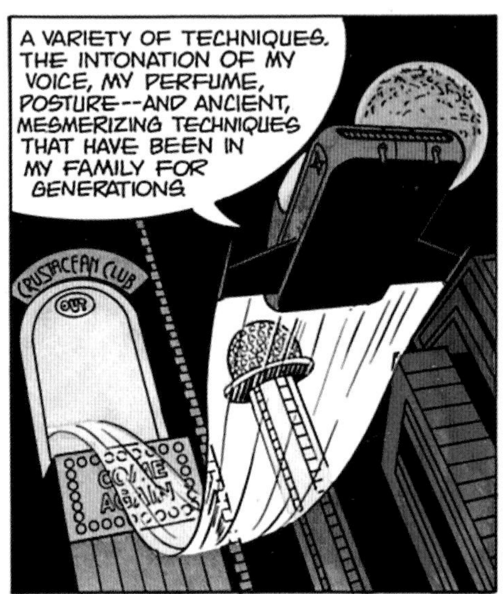
A VARIETY OF TECHNIQUES. THE INTONATION OF MY VOICE, MY PERFUME, POSTURE--AND ANCIENT, MESMERIZING TECHNIQUES THAT HAVE BEEN IN MY FAMILY FOR GENERATIONS.
CRUSTACEAN CLUB

FINALLY, IT IS THE WILL THAT MAKES IT HAPPEN. I WILL TEACH YOU THE TECHNIQUES. THE WILL YOU ALREADY HAVE.
YOU DON'T LIKE MEN DO YOU?
I NEITHER LIKE NOR DISLIKE. WELL? WILL YOU JOIN ME?

I'LL HAVE TO RETURN TO BASE, ARRANGE FOR A TRANSFER...
NO...

YOU WILL NOT GO BACK. I WILL HAVE YOUR THINGS FORWARDED. FROM THIS MOMENT ON, YOU ARE TWIG NUMBER ONE.
TCS
NEXT MONTH: SUNDRA'S FIRST MISSION!

S.RUDE '85
190 Proof
Saurian

THROW DOWN YOUR WEAPONS AND GIVE YOURSELF UP, RUTGER!
COME AND GET ME, HAMMER!
COPPERHEAD AMMO RANCH

IF I HAVE TO COME AND GET YOU, YOU'RE DEAD MEAT!
WHOOOOOOOOOSSHHH

ONE MORE CHANCE, RUTGER!
COME AND GET ME HAMMER!
G-T-7

FRAZZ

I SURRENDER, HAMMER!
TAKE ME BACK TO PRISON!
WHY YOU TAG-TEARING, MURDERING, THIEVING, ZAG-DEALING, LYING PIECE OF TRASH!
DON'T YOU UNDERSTAND INTERLAC?
THIS JOB PAYS DEAD OR ALIVE.
WE'RE DONE EARLY! SELBY--SET A COURSE FOR YLUM!
YOU CAN DO ANYTHING. BUT DON'T YOU STEP ON MY BLUE SUEDE SHOES!
2

BRIDGING INTERSTELLAR SPACE BY JUMPING THROUGH BLACK HOLES, THE HAMMERHEAD REACHES YLUM, HOME OF NEXUS.
BREAK OUT THE HATS AND WHISTLES! THE HAMMER COMES TO PARTY!

HOW'S BUSINESS, POP?
LARGE. WE HAVE A 250 CYCLE WAITING LIST. SUNDRA'S IN THE WEB NOW, BUYING MATERIALS TO INCREASE PRODUCTION.

HOW'S NEXUS?
I HAVE NOT SEEN HIM IN 10 CYCLES.

WHAT? IS HE HERE?
HE'S HERE. HE KEEPS TO HIMSELF. HIM AND HIS NEW FRIENDS.
WHAT FRIENDS?

FALSE FRIENDS. FLATTERERS AND PARASITES. AND WORSE.

HE WILL SEE ME--OR THERE WILL BE EXTENSIVE DAMAGE.
RALLY
CENTRAL CONCOURSE
WITH
PRESIDENT
TYRONE

GREAT NEXUS--ADMIT ME!
BAM
BAM

YAS?
WHERE IS NEXUS? DOES HE KNOW JUDAH MACCABEE IS HERE?
HISSSS
I'LL SEE...

PLEASE DON'T TROUBLE YOURSELF --I'LL SEE FOR MYSELF.
CRASH
3

NEXUS®

IS IT MY OLD FRIEND THE HAMMER? WHAT BRINGS YOU TO THIS GODFORSAKEN CINDER?

I THOUGHT YOUR GOD WAS EVERYWHERE.

NO... HIS ACHIEVEMENTS HAVE BEEN GREATLY EXAGGERATED.

HOLD STILL, BOSS. PLEASE?

INSOMNIA

MIKE BARON SCRIPT
STEVE RUDE PENCILS
ERIC SHANOWER INKS
STEVE HAYNIE LETTERS
LES DORSCHEID COLORS
RICK OLIVER EDITS

"Well look – if you damn guys are going to sit here and stare at me all night, I'm going to bed!"

Elvis Presley to the Beatles, 1964

WHO ARE THESE PEOPLE? WHY DO YOU SURROUND YOURSELF WITH LOUD COMPANY? YOU, WHO CRAVED SOLITUDE?
THEY ARE MY FRIENDS. THEY ACCEPT ME FOR WHAT I AM.
NARR--! FORK OVER, HI-BEAM!
YO-YO MA!
THE BOSS

AND WHAT MIGHT THAT BE?
A LOVER... A PHILOSOPHER... A STUDENT OF HISTORY.
COME...SIT... EAT...DRINK... WATCH VID WITH ME.
BOSS, I ONLY GOTS ONE MORE ADJUST-MENT...

AND THE DREAMS? WHAT OF THEM?
I NO LONGER DREAM.
ZAGBALL, HAMMER?
HOW IS THAT POSSIBLE?
I HAVE LEARNED TO CONTROL MY DREAMS.

ZAGBALLS?! THESE ARE POISON. I KILL ZAG DEALERS FOR A LIVING.

NONSENSE. ≥GULP≤ THEY'RE FUN IF YOU KNOW HOW TO CONTROL THEM.
GREAT GOULESSARIAN.
RELAX, MY FRIEND. WATCH THIS VID-- A MUSICAL. HOT OFF THE BOAT.

WHERE IS SUNDRA?
SHE BORES ME, MY ERSTWHILE LADY LOVE.
VID-3000
SHE TURNS OUT TO BE JUST ANOTHER PUSHY CAPITALIST --HER AND JIL-- LIKE A BEAST IN HEAT, THAT ONE.

YOU ARE BORED WITH SUNDRA? THEN YOU ARE BORED WITH LIFE.

THIS VID BORES ME...
5

VVWAP

WOGGA! WOGGA! THE BOSS JUST ZAPPED ANOTHER ONE!
SOMEBODY GO GET ANOTHER VID UNIT.

COME BACK TO EARTH WITH ME.
EARTH BORES ME.
BOSS, THAT WAS THE LAST VID.

THEN SEND OUT FOR ANOTHER ONE! JEEZUS! DO I HAVE TO DO EVERYTHING AROUND HERE?
NO SWEAT, BOSS!

GREAT NEXUS--COME WITH ME ON A TRAIL OF ADVENTURE...WE SHALL BRAVE TITAN'S WINDS, WE'LL...
YOU ARE BEGINNING TO BORE ME...

YASS...I CAN SEE WHERE MY COMPANY WOULD PROVE TEDIOUS FOR YOU...
THANKS FOR DROPPING BY.
BOSS--WANNA RACE FLOATERS UP AND DOWN THE FREIGHT CORRIDOR?
THE BOSS
6

G-7
DON'T FORGET THE RALLY TONITE
THOU ART IRRESISTABLE --FOR A HUMAN.
FLATTERER.
YOU'VE SEEN HIM?
AYE.
WHAT DO YOU THINK?
IT TEARS MY HEART. WHAT HAS HAPPENED?
AFTER THE LAST DREAM EXECUTION-- THE OLD GENERAL-- HE WAS DESPERATE.
SOMETHING HAPPENED TO HIM THERE --OR MAYBE IT'S BEEN BUILDING FOR A LONG TIME. HE RETURNED IN SECRET--HE HAD HIMSELF SURGICALLY ALTERED--
HOW?
"AN ELECTRODE IMPLANT. IT SHORT CIRCUITS HIS HEADACHES --AND GOD KNOWS WHAT ELSE.
"AND HE TAKES DRUGS TO PREVENT HIMSELF FROM SLEEPING."
I HAVE SEEN THE SIGNS. WHAT NOW?
I GO TO SEE HIM.
I'LL BE WITH DAVE.
7

SUNDRA! HAVE A ZAGBALL.
NO THANK YOU.
HORATIO...
HELLO, SUNDRA. WATCH VID WITH ME.

COULD I SEE YOU ALONE FOR A MINUTE?
THESE ARE MY FRIENDS. I HAVE NO SECRETS FROM THEM.

HORATIO, PLEASE...
BOSS--THE FLOATERS ARE READY!

GET THE HELL OUT OF HERE!
OKAY, OKAY! WHAT'S THE PROBLEM?

SHE'S BAD NEWS. ALL SHE DOES IS BUM HIM OUT.
YOU AIN'T WRONG.
YOU PROMISED ME YOU WOULDN'T HAVE THE OPERATION.
YOU DON'T KNOW WHAT IT'S LIKE BEING ME.

YOU'RE CHANGING--YOU'RE NOT THE MAN I FELL IN LOVE WITH.
LIFE IS CHANGE. I DO WHAT I MUST. THIS IS MY DESTINY.
IS IT YOUR DESTINY TO SIT SURROUNDED BY SYCOPHANTS, GORGING YOURSELD ON PROCESSED FOOD AND DRUGS? IGNORING YOUR FRIENDS? HURTING THOSE WHO LOVE YOU?
YOU DON'T UNDERSTAND A THING.
8

I GUESS NOT...

AHHHH...

DAVE'S PLACE.
MUNCH-MUNCH PASS THE THREE BEAN CURD, PLEASE...
BY ALL MEANS... GOBBLE LUTEFISK?

HE IS GONE, THE MAN I LOVED.
VERILY. I SUGGESTED FORCED THERAPY, BUT THE OLD MAN SAYETH NAY... LUTEFISK?

HE MUST WANT TO CHANGE. OUR WANTING HIM TO CHANGE WILL NOT AFFECT HIM.
I WOULD DIE FOR HIM. BUT I CANNOT WAIT FOR HIM.
I HAVE A LIFE OF MY OWN...

CHERNENKO--
HUB OF THE DWINDLING SOV EMPIRE.
COMRADE CHAIRMAN, COMRADE TWILLY HAS ARRIVED.
SEND HIM IN.

GREETINGS, COMRADE TWILLY. YOU HAVE BEEN CHOSEN FROM AMONG THE SOV'S ELITE AGENTS. ARE YOU PREPARED TO UNDERTAKE THIS ASSIGNMENT?
I AM, SUPREME COMMANDER.

NEXUS IS LIKE NO OTHER MILITARY TARGET. WE KNOW VERY LITTLE ABOUT HIM.
HE HAS MANAGED TO HARNESS FUSION ENERGY PERSONALLY --DOUBTLESS HE IS BACKED BY MANY SLAVE HEAD UNITS.
YOU WILL BE SIMILARLY EQUIPPED.

YOUR PARDON, SUPREME ONES --I PREFER TO FULFILL THIS MISSION BY MY OWN MEANS. I WILL NOT NEED THE FUSION HARNESS.

COMRADE, WE ARE COGNIZANT OF YOUR SKILLS. BUT NEXUS HAS TRANSCENDED MORTALITY. HE EMPLOYS A PERSONAL, CONSTANT, BIOLOGICALLY-BASED FORCE FIELD.
I AM AWARE OF THAT AND SO I HAVE PREPARED A DEMONSTRATION. WILL YOU REPAIR TO THE ARMORED TESTING CHAMBER? FOR YOUR OWN SAFETY. THE DEMONSTRATION IS UNSUITABLE FOR THESE ELEGANT ROOMS.
10

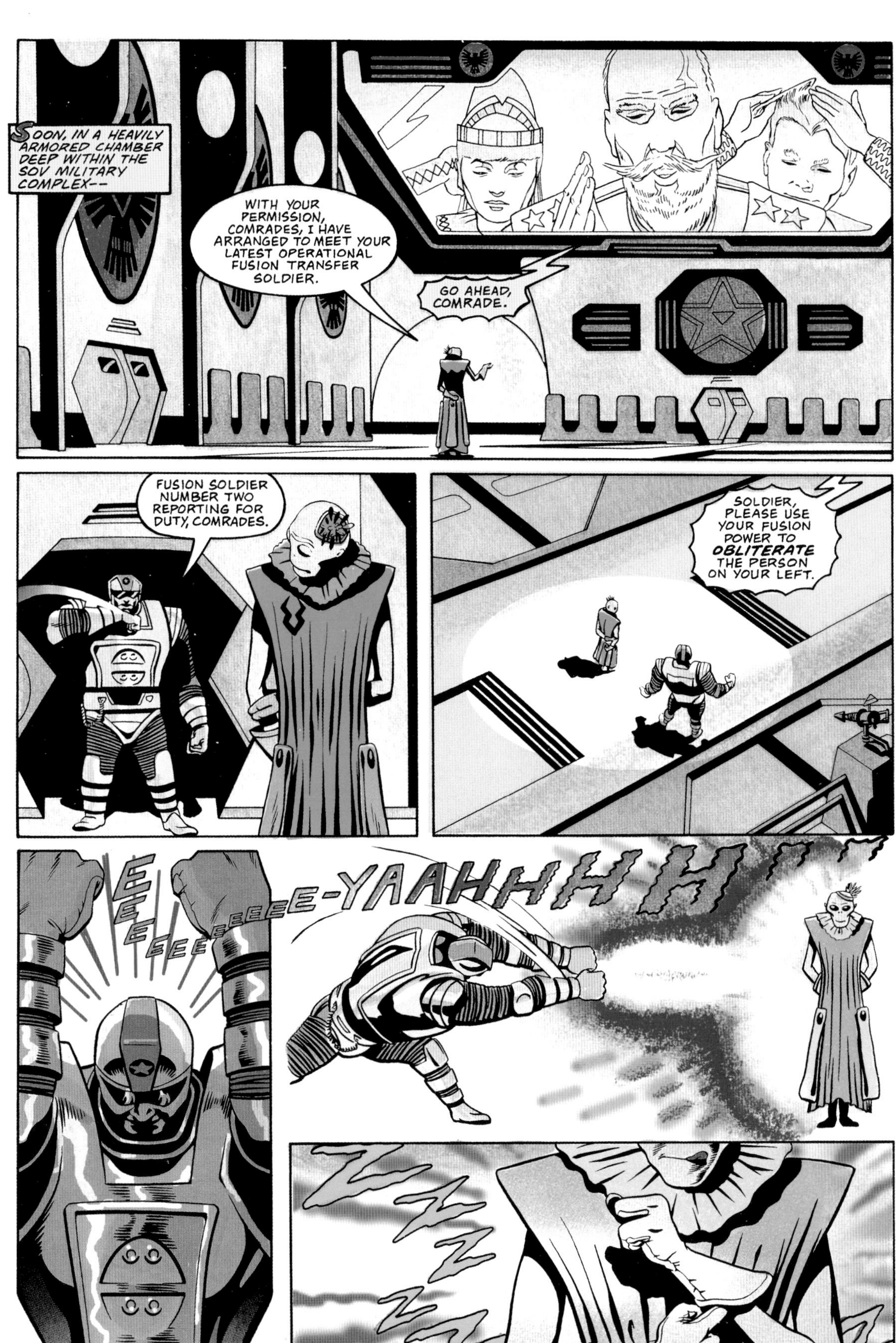
SOON, IN A HEAVILY ARMORED CHAMBER DEEP WITHIN THE SOV MILITARY COMPLEX--
WITH YOUR PERMISSION, COMRADES, I HAVE ARRANGED TO MEET YOUR LATEST OPERATIONAL FUSION TRANSFER SOLDIER.
GO AHEAD, COMRADE.
FUSION SOLDIER NUMBER TWO REPORTING FOR DUTY, COMRADES.
SOLDIER, PLEASE USE YOUR FUSION POWER TO OBLITERATE THE PERSON ON YOUR LEFT.
EEEEEEEEEEEEE-YAAHHHHH!!!!
11

CLICK

COMRADE TWILLY --HOW DID YOU DO THAT?
BY TURNING MYSELF INTO A TRANSFORMER AND CIRCUITING THE FUSION ENERGY BACK TO ITS SOURCE.

COMRADE CHAIRPERSONS-- FEEDBACK IS RIPPING THROUGH OUR TELEKASTERS --WE'RE TRYING TO SHUT DOWN WITHOUT CAUSING ANY MORE DAMAGE--
PULL THE PLUG!

THAT WILL RESULT IN A MASSIVE LOSS OF HEADS.
PULL IT!

A THOUSAND HEADS IS A SMALL PRICE, COMRADE. YOUR DEMONSTRATION IS MOST CONVINCING.
BY AVENGING OUR BELOVED GENERAL KROGH, YOU WILL FURTHER THE CAUSE OF INTERSTELLAR SOCIALISM.
YOU LEAVE FOR YLUM IN THREE DAYS.
COMRADES, I SHALL NOT FAIL.

AS SOON AS HE COMPLETES HIS MISSION, HE IS TO BE ELIMINATED.
HOW?
WE'RE WORKING ON IT.

S&J SOLAR BOAT WORKS, YLUM.
TAKE THOSE STABILIZER CIRCUITS TO DAVE, OKAY?
SURE.
TIK
TAK
TIK
TAKKA
TIK

HI, SUNNY ...
DON'T.

WHY NOT? THERE'S NOBODY HERE.
LET GO.

RAWWRR!!
13

HISSSSSSS
I'M SORRY--I NEVER WANT TO HURT YOU. BUT I MEAN IT-- DON'T TOUCH ME.
WHAT ABOUT THOSE TIMES IN THE SUNFLOWER? WHAT WAS THAT ALL ABOUT?
I DON'T KNOW. I'M NOT SORRY THEY HAPPENED. BUT RIGHT NOW, I HAVE TO BE BY MYSELF.
OKAY. I UNDERSTAND.
DON'T JUST SAY IT. BE MY FRIEND.
OKAY.
HORATIO--YOU SHOULD TURN THIS PLACE INTO A FUNBURG AND MAKE *ME* THE DIRECTOR.
YOU REALLY SHOULD AND I'LL TELL YOU WHY. GOGOLICK USED TO RUN THE FUNBURG ON DARTMOUTH, UNTIL THEY RAN HIM OFF. NOW HE'S WORTH MILLIONS.
TCB
YOU WANT ANOTHER ZAGBALL?
SURE, WHY NOT?

HEY HORATIO --CAN I HAVE A ZAGBALL?
NOPE. SORRY, KID. STUNT YOUR GROWTH.

NEW VIDS ARE IN!
LET'S SEE 'EM!
GIMME!

TWO ON ONE PART THREE!
HEAVENS TO MURGATROID! --THE UNEXPURGATED VERSION!
HEY KRONK-- YOU'RE STEPPING ON HORATIO'S ROBE.
OOPS, SORRY.

HEY HORATIO-- CAN I HAVE ONE OF THESE LITTLE STATUES?
SURE, WHY NOT?

VREEE VREEEEEE
WHAT'S THIS?
MACBETH, BY BAD BOB AND HIS SUPPLY SIDE NEBULONS.
ALIENS CAN'T DO SHAKESPEARE. GET THAT SMOKE OUT OF MY FACE.

SURE THEY CAN! NEXT THING, YOU'LL SAY HUMANS CAN'T SING THE PINKS.
THIS IS GARBAGE, CAN WE TALK?
VREEE
HEY, GIVE IT A CHANCE--!

BOO-OOM
GARBAGE!
WANNNGG
WHOOP!
15

I'LL SET UP ANOTHER VID.
WOGGA-WOGGA! THE BOSS JUST ZAPPED ONE!
VVRREEEEE
WHAT IS THAT INFERNAL CACOPHONY?
THE BOSS
VOOPER

IT'S ME, HORATIO.
WHAT IS THIS THING?
I DON'T KNOW--SOME KIND OF MUSICAL INSTRUMENT I FOUND IN THE RUINS.
CAN I HAVE IT?
SURE, WHY NOT?

HEY MEZZ--I'LL GIVE YOU ◬1000 FOR THAT BEAT-UP OLD THING. YOU CAN BUY YOURSELF A REAL GEOTAR.
NO THANKS.

IS NEXUS IN?
NOPE, SORRY. MAYBE TOMORROW. WANT TO LEAVE A MESSAGE?
DAVE!

KRONK--LET HIM IN! YOU CAN'T KEEP HIM OUT! THAT'S DAVE!
TCB
THANKEE, BR'ER MEZZROW.

WHAT'S ON VID?
WE'RE GOING TO WATCH SOME MASSACRES AND ATROCITIES FROM THE ARGENTO-LATHAM WAR. SOON AS GOGOLICK GETS THE VID SET UP.
SOUNDS FABULOUS. MAY I STAY?
SURE, WHY NOT?
16

WHERE'S GOGOLICK? WHY ISN'T THE VID SET UP? DO I HAVE TO DO EVERYTHING MYSELF AROUND HERE?

HORATIO--FORGET THAT SAP! I GOT SOME SIZZLIN' FLOATERS READY TO GO.
SURE, WHAT THE HELL. LET'S RUMBLE.
VOOPER

RUMBLE?
WE GOT SOME SOUPED-UP FLOATERS AND A SERVICE CORRIDOR THAT WRAPS CLEAR AROUND THE PLANET LIKE A HOOLA-HOOP. 1500 KM FLAT OUT. COME ON --IT'S FUN.
SOUNDS HAZARDOUS.
TCB

OF COURSE IT'S HAZARDOUS! THAT'S WHY WE DO IT. COME ON--YOU CAN RIDE WITH ME.

THIS LITTLE BABY HAS A MICRO-MELT DRIVING A STEAM ENGINE--SHE'LL DO MACH ONE IN HERE.

OUTTA THE WAY, ROAD-HOGS!
ZOOM
17

NO ONE PASSES ME!

GREAT GOULESSARIAN! KRONK HIT THE WALL! STOP!
KRONK CAN LOOK OUT FOR HIMSELF.

IF YOU VALUE MY FRIENDSHIP, TURN THIS THING AROUND.

HA HA! I'LL BEAT GREAT NEXUS!

PUT OUT THE FIRE.

KRONK IS DEAD.
THAT'S TOO BAD. HE SHOULD HAVE WORN A FORCE FIELD.

WE MUST TAKE THE BODY BACK TO CENTRAL...
NO WE DON'T --STAND ASIDE.

COME ON. MAYBE THOSE DUMMIES GOT THE VID SET UP.

IS THAT VID WORKING YET?
YOU BETCHA! GOT A NEW LOAD OF ZAGBALLS, TOO! SOME RIGHTEOUS MIX, BOSS.
19

THIS WILL BOOST YOU INTO ORBIT.
DAVE-- WHERE YOU GOING?
I HAVE WORK. GOOD DAY.
WHAT A STIFF!
HEY, FORGET THAT LOSER. RELAX--DO SOME ZAG--CHECK OUT THE NEW VIDS.
HERE'S ONE THAT CAME SPECIAL, JUST FOR YOU.
KILLING JOKE
featuring
CLONEZONE
THE HILARIATOR™
NEXT MONTH

THE GRAB
MIKE BARON STORY
ERIC SHANOWER ART & LETTERS
LES DORSCHEID COLORS
RICK OLIVER EDITS
FOR MILLENIA, THE MYSTERIOUS BEACONS OF SARED-JYN HAVE GUIDED SEAFARING TRAVELLERS IN AND OUT OF DEL BAY. LEGEND HAS IT THAT SHOULD ANYTHING EVER HAPPEN TO THE BEACONS, A GREAT DISASTER WOULD BEFALL THE CITY OF SARED-JYN.
THERE IT IS, CREW. BUOY JORJ--THE APOGEE OF THE SARED-JYN RACECOURSE.
ONCE AROUND THE BEACON, THEN HARD ABOUT AND A BEELINE FOR THE YACHT CLUB. THE WINDS ARE VERY TRICKY HERE.
THEY DON'T SEEM TRICKY.
OF COURSE NOT, SUNDRA. WE'RE IN A POWER LAUNCH. BUT WAIT UNTIL TOMORROW. YOU'LL SEE.
CINDROID'S RIGHT. THE WINDS ARE A BITCH ON RACE DAY. NEVER FAILS. WITHOUT THE BEACONS, THEY SAY IT WOULD BE WORSE.
YOU MEAN THE BEACONS ACTUALLY AFFECT THE WIND?
SO LEGEND HAS IT.
1.

NOT SO MUCH THE WIND AS THE CURRENTS. THEY SAY THAT WITHOUT THE BEACONS, TERRIBLE WHIRLPOOLS WOULD MAKE THE HARBOR UNNAVIGABLE.
THE BEST PRACTICE FOR THE REGATTA IS JUST SAILING THE SARED SEA. OR SO THEY SAY.

WHO SAYS?
SEERS, SAGES, AND SAVANTS. ALSO SOLDIERS, SAILORS AND SALT WATER SAINTS.
SSSSS--!

OKAY, CREW, LISTEN UP. WE'VE GOT A BIG DAY TOMORROW--SO EVERYBODY GET A GOOD NIGHT'S SLEEP. MEET ME AT THE PIER PRECISELY AT SIX.
AYE-AYE, CAPTAIN BLUE.

SO, SUN, YOU WANT TO HAVE DINNER AND CRASH AT MY PLACE?
LEAD ON, CINDROID. YOU'RE MY NATIVE GUIDE. BUT WATCH THE ALLITERATION AND BAD PUNS!

THIS RACE MEANS THE WORLD TO CAPTAIN BLUE.
HOW LONG HAVE YOU KNOWN HIM?

ALL MY LIFE, I GUESS. HE'S AN OLD FRIEND OF THE FAMILY. IN FACT, YOU'RE THE ONLY CREWMEMBER HE HASN'T KNOWN FOR AT LEAST SEVERAL YEARS.
I'M THE ONLY ONE WHO EARNED A PLACE THROUGH SHEER SKILL, YES?

YOU NEVER WOULD HAVE MADE IT WITHOUT MY STERLING ENDORSEMENT.
YEAH? WELL, YOU DIDN'T KNOW WHAT A MILKSHAKE WAS UNTIL I CAME ALONG, SO WE'RE EVEN.
2.

TELL ME ABOUT THE PLACE YOU COME FROM.
MARS? IT'S NOT MUCH. SARED-JYN IS SO MUCH MORE BEAUTIFUL. I WISH I'D BEEN BORN HERE.
AND I WISH I COULD TRAVEL THE STARS LIKE YOU. OH, SUNDRA-- I'D GIVE ANYTHING TO DO WHAT YOU DO--

JUST TRAVELLING, RELYING ON MY SKILLS, MY PLUCK AND MY LUCK...
BETTY'S DEPT

SENDING MY EXPERIENCES HOME FOR OTHERS TO ENJOY...

GO TO SLEEP NOW. WE'VE GOT A BUSY DAY AHEAD.
GOODNIGHT, SUNDRA. THANKS FOR BEING MY FRIEND.

THE NEXT DAY--
OKAY, CREW, THIS IS IT. WE'RE GOING TO SAIL THIS COURSE SO FAST, THE OTHER 35 ENTRIES WILL THINK THEY'VE RUN AGROUND.
THIS IS MY NINTH REGATTA. I'VE FINISHED SECOND TWICE AND FOURTH ONCE.

BUT THIS IS THE FIRST REGATTA FOR ***OUR*** SHIP, THE ***LOVELY LUCILLE***. SHE HAS BEEN CLOCKED FASTER THAN ANY OTHER CLASS 'D' YACHT ON THIS PLANET.

SHE'S THE MEANEST, LEANEST LITTLE LADY IN THE FLEET! SHE'S FLY, SHE'S SPRY, SHE'S HONEY-SWEET! FLOAT LIKE A BUTTERFLY, STING LIKE A BEE!
3.

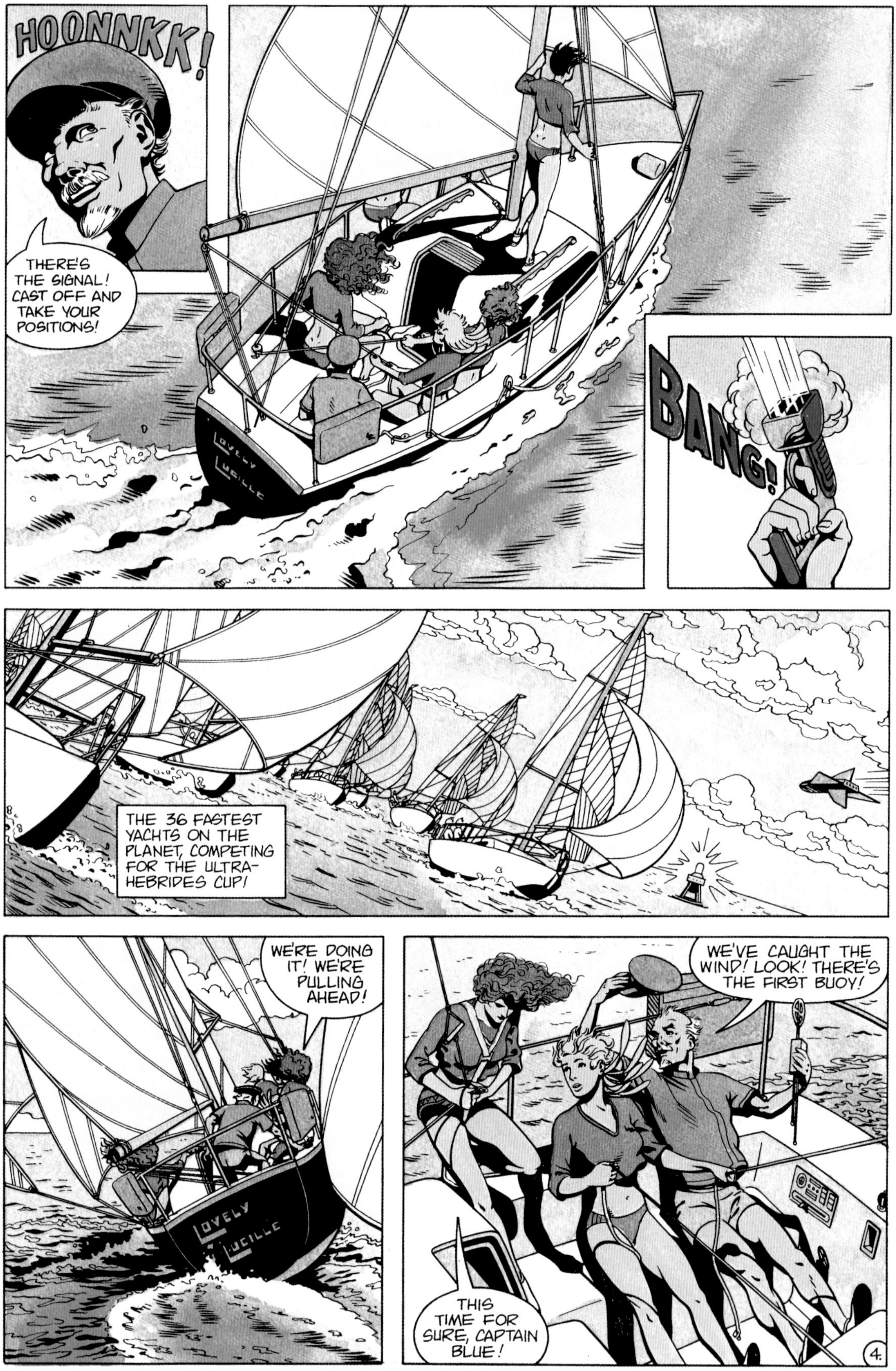

HOONNKK!

THERE'S THE SIGNAL! CAST OFF AND TAKE YOUR POSITIONS!

LOVELY LUCILLE

BANG!

PORT--NINETEEN DEGREES! PREPARE TO COME ABOUT!
LOVELY LUCILLE

COME ABOUT!

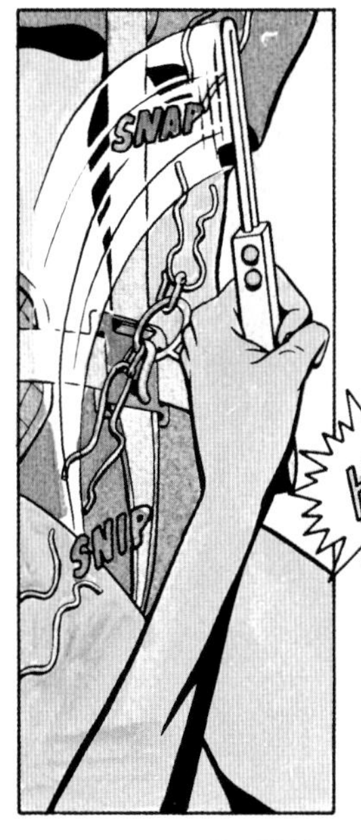
SNAP
SNIP

HEY!

MAN OVER-BOARD!

HANG ON, CINDROID!
5.

YOU OKAY?
YES-- (GASP!)
JUST LET YOURSELF GO LIMP. I'M HEADING FOR THE BUOY.
NOW JUST PULL YOURSELF UP.
IT'S AGAINST THE LAW (GASP!) FOR ANYONE TO EVEN **TOUCH** THE BUOYS!
I KNOW THAT. THIS IS AN **EMERGENCY.**
WHAT ARE YOU DOING? THAT'S NOT A LIFE-RAFT.
IT'S A PORTABLE TELEPORTATION NET.
GRAB THE OTHER SIDE AND PULL IT DOWN.
WHY? WHAT ARE YOU **DOING?**
WE'RE GETTING OUT OF HERE. IT'S OKAY-- SUNDRA TO MOTHER HEN. LAY AN EGG.
BLINK!
PERFECT.
SUNDRA, WHERE ARE WE? I DON'T UNDERSTAND!
6.

YOU'RE ABOARD A **WEB BATTLESHIP** ORBITING THE PLANET. THE WEB NEEDS **ENERGY** SO WE'RE BORROWING ONE OF YOUR BEACONS. THIS IS MY BOSS, COMMANDER IMADA.
WE REGRET THIS INCONVENIENCE. YOU WILL BE RETURNED TO SARED-JYN SHORTLY.

INCONVENIENCE ?! OH, SUNDRA-- YOU DON'T KNOW WHAT YOU'VE DONE! LOOK TO THE HARBOR!

OH COME ON--THAT'S JUST AN ANCIENT SUPERSTITION.
IS IT ?! TURN ON YOUR VIEWSCREENS! **LOOK TO THE HARBOR!**

CLICK!

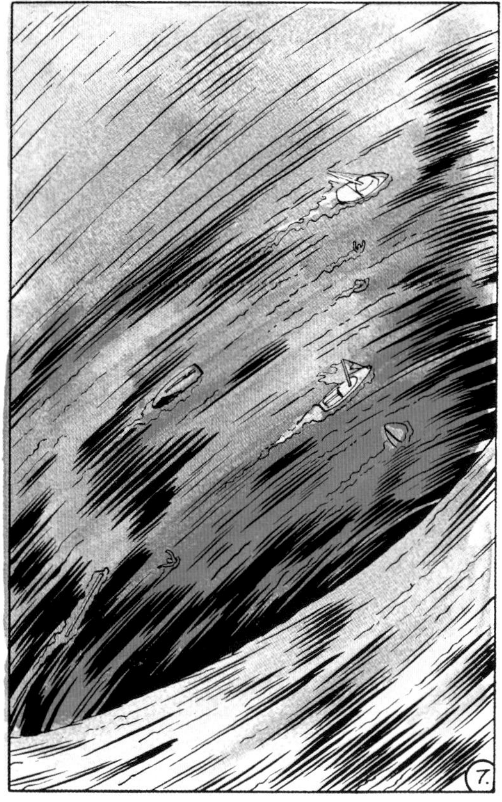
7.

AWOOGAH
AWOOGAH
CAPTAIN BLUE--ALL MY FRIENDS--
ATTENTION, ALL CREW, THIS IS YOUR CAPTAIN SPEAKING. PRIME FOR WEB. JUMP IN TEN MINUTES.

STEVE
RUDE

KILLING JOKE
NEXUS®
MIKE BARON SCRIPT
STEVE RUDE PENCILS
ERIC SHANOWER INKS
STEVE HAYNIE LETTERS
LES DORSCHEID COLORS
RICK OLIVER EDITS
WHAT DO YOU MEAN, "OFF LIMITS?" I CREATED THIS WORLD!
GET OUT OF MY WAY!
TCB
Happy the dumb beast, hungering for food
But calling not his suffering his own.
——Santayana
SORRY, SIR. NO ONE CAN BE ADMITTED WITHOUT EXPRESS PERMISSION OF PRESIDENT TYRONE.
STAND ASIDE, DROOG, OR YOU'RE GOING TO GET HURT.
THE BOSS

WE KNOW WHO YOU ARE, SIR. WE STILL CANNOT ADMIT YOU WITHOUT PRESIDENT TYRONE'S PERMISSION.
OKAY DROOG. YOU ASKED FOR IT.
SQUAT

SWAK
BOSS

I'M VERY SORRY, SIR. BUT NO ONE CAN BE ADMITTED WITHOUT...

WOOUGH

OUCH!
HOLD IT RIGHT THERE!
I GOT HIM, KREED ...

THAK!
BZZT! BZZT!
I...I GOT HIM, GODDAMN IT!

ZONK
IT'S GONE.

GREAT NEXUS GOES WHERE HE PLEASES.
CITIZEN!
3

CITIZEN, I'M SURPRISED TO FIND YOU IN THE MIDDLE OF THIS FRACAS.
IT'S GONE ≷GIGGLE≶.
YOU HAD BETTER COOL IT, MY FRIEND!
TCB

WHAT DO YOU MEAN? WHAT'S GONE?
THE POWER... HA HA HA! THE DAMNED THING!
TCB

GOOD JOB, YOU MEN! CARRY ON.
GREAT NEXUS WILL REMEMBER. AND IF HE DOES NOT, I SHALL DO IT FOR HIM.
KREED-- DON'T YOU SEE? HA HA HA! IT'S GONE!

COME ON, GREAT ONE. LET'S GO.
HA HA HA!
WE SHOWED THEM!

WHAT'S IT ALL ABOUT, SWERDLOW?
MANY THINGS, MR. PRESIDENT. CLEARLY, GREAT NEXUS IS IN THE GRIP OF SOME MALADY ...YOU KNOW HE HAD HIMSELF ALTERED...
I'D HEARD.
A TRAGEDY.
TERRIBLE.
BUT THE FOUR-ARMED ONE--KREED. THERE IS TROUBLE.
WHAT TO DO, SWERDLOW? WHAT TO DO?
4

SO. THE DREAM HAS PASSED.
UHH?
LEAVE ME.
HEY, YOU DON'T WANT TO BE ALONE, DO YOU BOSS?
YES. GET OUT. EVERYONE.
HEH HEH HEH ...ALL GONE ...HEH HEH...
DREAM'S OVER! EVERYBODY OFF! HEH HEH HEH...
YOU KNOW I'M SO LONELY, YOU KNOW I'M SO LONELY...
GO AHEAD, HEH HEH... MAKE MY DAY...
I'M SO LONELY, I COULD DIE...
KLIK
VID-3000
KILLING JOKE
CLONEZONE!

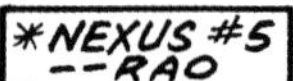

HERE I AM! GIVE ME MONEY --I'LL MAKE YOU LAUGH!

GREETINGS.

GREETINGS AND SALUTATIONS FROM **HOTCHKISS**. YOU WILL NOT MAKE ME LAUGH FOR I AM...

FOUL! FOUL! YOU'RE A **MINEHEAD!** I MOST HEARTILY PROTEST! MINEHEADS ARE DEPRIVED OF THE LAUGHING GENE! I **CAN'T** MAKE YOU LAUGH!

TRUE. BUT YOU'RE NOT SUPPOSED TO MAKE **ME** LAUGH--I AM A MESSENGER, A REPRESENTATIVE OF HOTCHKISS. IT IS **HE** WHOM YOU MUST FRACTURE WITH FRIVOLITIES.

HOTCHKISS IS **HUMAN**.

GREAT.

HUMANS ARE A **CINCH!** THEY SAY **JACK BENNY** WAS A HUMAN--

PERSONALLY I BELIEVE HE WAS PART LIZIGATOR.

YOUR QUARTERS, HILARIATOR.

MAKE YOURSELF COMFORTABLE. WE REACH HOTCHKISS' PLACE IN 39 HOURS.

VID

SAY--THIS HOTCHKISS KNOWS HOW TO TREAT A CELEBRITY.

6

THANK ALVIN THIS HOTCHKISS IS HUMAN! THEY'RE THE EASIEST TO MAKE LAUGH. THEY PRACTICALLY INVENTED HUMOR.
WE LIZIGATORS MERELY REFINED IT.
FLY ME TO THE MOOOON--- AND LET ME GAZE UPON THE STARRSS---
WE DOCK IN NINE MINUTES, SIR. I MUST NOW INFORM YOU OF CERTAIN CONDITIONS ATTENDING THIS CONTRACT...
CONDITIONS? WHAT CONDITIONS?
THOUGH ONE OF THE WEALTHIEST MEN IN THE CIVILIZED GALAXY, HOTCHKISS SUFFERS FROM AN UNFORTUNATE AFFLICTION--HE HAS NOT LAUGHED IN 25 YEARS.
NOT SO MUCH AS A CHUCKLE.
HE IS DESPERATE TO LAUGH. HE WILL KILL TO LAUGH. HE HAS KILLED TO LAUGH.
THE LAST 29 HILARIATORS I HAVE PROCURED FAILED TO RAISE EVEN A FAINT SMILE...
THEY WERE EJECTED INTO SPACE. THEY DIED IN AGONY! BUT IT WAS QUICK!
SHOULD YOU FAIL TO MAKE HOTCHKISS LAUGH, YOU WILL BE EJECTED INTO SPACE!
AND WHATEVER YOU DO, DO NOT--REPEAT: DO NOT MENTION HIS NOSE!!
7

HEY MINEHEAD--I'M AN ENTERTAINER, NOT A PSYCHO-SHOCK THERAPIST! NO SIGNEE CONTRACT, NO GOTS TO DO THE SHOW. JUST PAY ME MY USUAL, UH, KILL FEE, AND UH, LET ME OFF AT THE NEAREST CIVILIZED PORT.
THERE IS NO TURNING BACK, MR. CLONEZONE. WE ARE DOCKING. PLEASE GATHER YOUR PERSONAL EFFECTS AND FOLLOW ME.
HEY, I GET IT! MY OLD PAL MURPHMAN PUT YOU UP TO THIS, RIGHT? IT'S A GAG, RIGHT? RIGHT?
HOTCHKISS
GREAT ZOT! JOKIN' JOHNNY JERKOWITZ COULDN'T MAKE HIM LAUGH? ≥GULP!≤ I ALWAYS WONDERED WHAT HAPPENED TO JOKIN' JOHN.
HOTCHKISS AWAITS THROUGH YONDER PORTAL.
DON'T I GET A WARM-UP ACT OR ANYTHING?
GO!
CLIK!
ZAP
ZOOM
AH, MR. HOTCHKISS? I'M FROM ACTORS EQUITY --I'VE COME IN PERSON TO EXPLAIN WHY CLONEZONE COULDN'T BE HERE.
COME CLOSER.

AM I CLOSE ENOUGH? I JUST WANT TO EXPLAIN ABOUT THE MIX-UP, THEN I'LL BE ON MY WAY...
TAKE YOUR HANDS DOWN.
GLEEP!
WELL?
THAT'S, THAT'S A DEEP SUBJECT ...
ARE YOU TRYING TO BE FUNNY?
NO, NO... AS I SAID-- I AM NOT THE HILARIATOR ...
EXCUSE ME ...DIDN'T MEAN TO BUMP YOUR ...YOUR...
I SEE.
MINEHEAD! THROW THIS RASCAL OUT THE AIRLOCK!
WAITAMINUTE! WAITAMINUTE!

WELL?
UH... UH...
OH HELL.
WHY DON'T YOU JUST INSTALL A SKI-LIFT AND MAKE A FEW BUCKS OFF THAT THING?
WHAT?
MAY I SPEAK FRANKLY?
THIS PRODIGIOUS PROBOSCIS IS BOUND TO DOMINATE DISCOURSE AMONG THINKING CREATURES...
BUMPITY BUMPITY
BUMPITY
WE'RE TALKING NASAL OBSERVATORY HERE--BEND OVER FAR ENOUGH AND YOU CAN SEE URANUS...
LEMME JUST PUT A SHINE ON THE SLOPES FOR YA-- DON'T AIM IT AT ANYTHING COMBUSTIBLE...
WIPE WIPE WIPE
SQUEAK SQUEAK
KNOW WHAT YOU REMIND ME OF?
THE MUTANT OFFSPRING OF NIXON AND A DEEP SPACE PROBE. YOU OUGHTA BE ON VID! SINCERELY.

HOTCHKISS, I KNOW HOW YOU FEEL. NANETTE FABRAY I AIN'T!
ON THE OTHER HAND, I DON'T HAVE TO CARRY A BED SHEET IN MY HIP POCKET!
LET ME GIVE YOU SOME ADVICE--DON'T GO OUT WITH YOUR COLLAR UP, THEY'LL ARREST YOU FOR INDECENT EXPOSURE.
WOULD YOU LOOK AT THE TIME! I'M DUE IN SURGERY IN NINE CYCLES! I'M TRANSPLANTING THE BRAIN OF AN ARMADILLO INTO THE BODY OF A SENATOR! WE HOPE TO CREATE A MORE INTELLIGENT SENATOR.
HEH --
GOTTA RUN! CIAO, BABY! WATCH WHERE YOU SWING THAT THING!
HEH HEH HEH--
CHOKE--!
GASP--!
SO THIS GUY GOES INTO THE MEDIVAC --DOC, HE SAYS, I GOT A TERRIBLE TAPEWORM...
NO--! GASP! WHEEZE --!
YES! DOC TELLS HIM TO COME BACK THE NEXT DAY WITH TWO APPLES AND A COOKIE...

NEXT DAY, GUY COMES BACK, DOC TELLS HIM TO DROP HIS PANTS...
NO--! PLEASE --!
AH HAHAHAHAHEEHOOOHO
NEXT DAY, SAME THING. GOES ON FOR A WEEK! GUY'S GOING NUTS! DOC, HE SAYS. HOW LONG DOES THIS GO ON?
DOC TELLS HIM TO DROP HIS PANTS AND BEND OVER! SHOVES THE TWO APPLES AND THE COOKIE UP THE GUY'S BUNG HOLE... DOC TELLS HIM TO COME BACK TOMORROW, BRING TWO APPLES AND A COOKIE...
WE'RE ALMOST THROUGH, DOC TELLS HIM. TOMORROW, BRING TWO APPLES AND A HAMMER.
NEXT DAY, THE DOC SHOVES THE TWO APPLES UP THE GUY'S BUNG HOLE--STANDS THERE WITH THE HAMMER.
PRETTY SOON, TAPEWORM STICKS ITS HEAD OUT AND GROWLS...
"WHERE THE HELL'S MY COOKIE?!" WHAM!
GASPPPPPPPPP
THAT HOTCHKISS HAD QUITE A SENSE OF HUMOR... AND HE CARRIED A LOT OF CASH.
HE WAS ONE HELL OF A SWEET GUY, I KID YOU NOT. 1000, 1001, 1002...
12

MEZZ! WHAT IT IS! SOME SWOG SOUNDS COMIN' OUT THAT THING.

HAIL, TONY.
BROUGHT MY SAX.
GET IT OUT AND GET IT ON.

JAXON'S GOING TO POUND SOME SKINS.
VOOTIE!
BEAT IT
SWOG MY HOG.

SPACEWALK WITH SOME RADIATED HOT SAUCE, KEY OF F♭, PENTATONIC SCALE.
JAXON, PUT A GLIDE ON THAT...
VOOTIE.

13

IN THE GREAT HALL, TYRONE CONDUCTS NEW CITIZENS THROUGH THE SWEARING-IN CEREMONY.
INCIPIENT CITIZENS-- GREETINGS!
YOUR PROBATIONARY PERIOD IS OVER AND YOU ARE READY TO PLUNGE HEADFIRST INTO THE WORLD OF TOMORROW, HERE ON THE VERY FRONTIER OF SPACE AND TIME!
YES, I SAY UNTO YOU-- GREETINGS!

TIME TO TAKE THE OATH OF CITIZENSHIP! I TRUST YOU ALL CAN UNDERSTAND ME -- THE TRANSLATORS ARE WORKING--
PSST! CLAUDE-- GET RID OF THAT SUCKER!
WHICH ONE?
THE LOLLIPOP, YOU--!

THEREFORE, AND WITH DUE CEREMONY, PLEASE RAISE YOUR LEFT APPENDAGE...

THOSE WITHOUT A LEFT APPENDAGE MAY SIMPLY LEAN... AND REPEAT AFTER ME... I, TYRONE...

SVI-SVIMMMEEEEEEE--

I LURKER ...
I STRUTHIO-MIMUS...

I, TWILLY...
14

PLEDGE ALLEGIANCE TO THE PLANET YLUM AND DO SOLEMLY SWEAR TO UPHOLD THE PRINCIPLES OF THE CONSTITUTION--TO DEAL FAIRLY AND RESPECTFULLY WITH ALL LIVING THINGS AND TO PROTECT THE PHYSICAL PLANT FROM VANDALISM OR ABUSE...
...SO HELP ME GOD.

HI, SUNDRA!
HI, MEZZ. WHAT'S HAPPENING?

TONY AND I ARE WORKING ON A SOUND. NEXUS GAVE ME A ZITAR!

LATER!
STAY OUTTA TROUBLE.

NEXUS IS SICK, ISN'T HE?
YES.
WHAT ARE WE GOING TO DO?

I'VE TRIED EVERYTHING... BUT WHEN YOU LOVE SOMEONE, SOMETIMES THAT ISN'T ENOUGH.
BUT HE LOVES YOU. YOU COULD GET HIM TO STOP TAKING THE DRUGS ...
15

I HAVE TRIED. I WOULD SAVE HIM IF I COULD. BUT HE DOESN'T WANT ME AROUND.
IT'S THOSE GRINKS AND GROINKS HE HANGS OUT WITH! THEY KEEP HIM SO HYPED ON ZAG HE DOESN'T KNOW WHO HE IS!

NO, MEZZ-- THEY'RE ONLY A SYMPTOM.
YOU KNEW HORATIO WHEN HE WAS WHOLE. DO YOU HONESTLY BELIEVE HE WOULD PERMIT THAT GANG OF LOSERS TO CONTROL HIM?
NO...I GUESS NOT

THEN PRAY FOR HIM. PRAY TO THAT GOD WHOM HE WORSHIPS. I'LL SEE YOU LATER.

WHAT IT IS.
ENTER.
WHAT DO YOU THINK ABOUT MARS? PLENTY OF SKILLED LABOR, TAX INCREMENTAL FUNDING, READY AVAILABILITY OF PARTS...
VID SCAN
enter

IT MAKES SENSE. YOU SHOULD MOVE THE FACTORY.
"BUT." DO I HEAR A "BUT" IN THERE?

NO BUTS. I DO NOT CLAIM TO UNDERSTAND THE WORKINGS OF THE HUMAN HEART. I MAKE NO JUDGMENT. YOU ARE MY FRIEND, REGARDLESS. BUT I WON'T JOIN YOU. THIS IS MY HOME NOW.
I DIDN'T THINK YOU'D LEAVE.
I LIKE IT HERE.

16

YOU WILL OF COURSE RETAIN FULL PARTNERSHIP, DRAW SALARY AND PARTICIPATE IN BOARD MEETINGS.
NONSENSE.
YOU WILL.
OF COURSE.
WOGGA! THROW ALL FOUR!
WOGGA! FOUR AT ONCE!
NO ONE IS GREATER THAN KREED!
COMRADE KREED?
COMRADE TWILLY. SOV REFUGEE.
I UNDERSTAND WE SHARE A COMMON INTEREST IN EXOTIC HAND WEAPONS...

WHAT CAN YOU SHOW ME?
I WAS SEARCHED COMING IN OF COURSE, SO I'VE HAD TO IMPROVISE. DO YOU KNOW THE TRICK WITH THE COLORED SHINGLES?
G-HYUK-- G-HYUK--

EVERY CHILD ON YLUM KNOWS HOW TO KILL WITH COLORED SHINGLES.
SNATCH

YOU HAVE NOTHING TO SHOW ME.
TAKE GOOD CARE OF MY INCENDIARY MITES.

YOU'RE BLUFFING! THEY COULDN'T PASS THE METAL SCREEN...

I RAISED THEM FROM SINGLE CELLS. I BROUGHT THEM IN MY RETINA--DID YOU KNOW I HAVE METALLIC RETINAS?
STAND VERY STILL AND I'LL CALL THEM OUT...

ZIP ZIP ZIP ZIP ZIP ZIP ZIP ZIP ZIP ZIP ZIP ZIP ZIP

POP POP POP POP

YOU HAVE MY ATTENTION, COMRADE.
I UNDERSTAND YOU KNOW GREAT NEXUS...
18

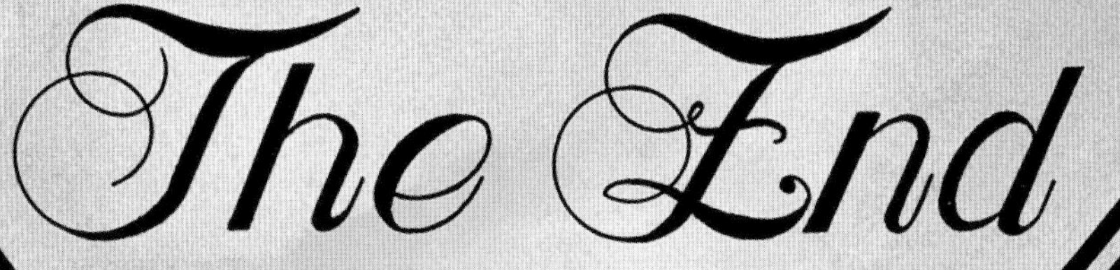
The End
LOOK FOR KILLING E II COMING SOON TO
VID-O-M NEAR YOU.
HEH HEH HEH...
..."THE MUTANT OFFSPRING OF NIXON AND A DEEP SPACE PROBE!"
HEH HEH HEH...

ZONE, YOU DEVIL! I WISH YOU WERE HERE!
WHERE THE...WHERE THE HELL IS EVERYBODY?!

HELLO?! SONS OF BITCHES RAN OUT ON ME! SONS OF BITCHES... HELLO?!

I NEED SOME ZAG!

DO I HAVE TO DO EVERYTHING MYSELF AROUND HERE?!
AH, HERE IT IS ...
BOSS

GOTTA GET STRAIGHT-- SNORT GOTTA...
HORATIO...

YOU'VE GONE TOO FAR, HORATIO.
WE'VE COME TO SET YOU STRAIGHT ...
ALPH? BETA? NO... NO!
NEXT
YOU ASKED FOR IT!

SOMEWHERE FAR FROM NEW YORK.
CLONEZONE
THE HILARIATOR
TM
The Office of Opportunity
MIKE BARON SCRIPT
MARK A. NELSON ART
STEVE HAYNIE LETTERS
LES DORSCHEID COLORS
RICK OLIVER EDITS
IF I CAN MAKE IT THERE-- I'LL MAKE IT ANYWHERE...
SO HERE'S TO YOUUUU--- NEW YORK--
NEWWW YORRRRRK!!
CLAP-CLAP
ZZZZ-- HUNH? MFFGZZ...
THANK YOU, MERCI, GRACIAS...
GOOD SHOW, ZONE. SORRY ABOUT THE HOUSE.
THAT'S ALL RIGHT, YORGA. I'M USED TO IT. JUST GIVE ME MY GUARANTEE AND I'M GONE.

AH, SPOT OF BOTHER THERE, ZONE. THE OWNER SPLIT FOR PARTS UNKNOWN DURING INTERMISSION AND TOOK ALL THE CASH RECEIPTS.
OH NO-- YOU'RE NOT CHEATING ME OUT OF MY FEE!
HE LEFT ME HIGH AND DRY TOO!
YOU LITTLE WEASEL! YOU'RE THE GUY WHO CONTRACTED ME!
CAUSE NO FRICTION, GET NO HURT!
ZONE, SWEETIE-- I WOULDN'T LEAVE YOU WITH AN EMPTY TANK!
HERE--TAKE THIS HOME COMPUTER! USE IT TO MANAGE YOUR FINANCES! IT'S WORTH ₳500, AT LEAST.
THANKS, YORGA. JUST WHAT I NEEDED.
DUM DE DUM-- BORN UNDER A BAD SIGN--
ALAS, TRAGEDY HAS STRUCK--AND THE BEREAVED ARE PROVIDING FOOD AND DRINK... 'TIS AN OLD TITAN CUSTOM...
MY DEEPEST SYMPATHIES FOR YOUR GRIEVOUS LOSS...
DENK CHOO.
2

EAT IT, EAT IT-- GO ON AND TAKE AN EGG AND BEAT IT--

MY SINCEREST CONDOLENCES ⇒MUNCH, CHEW⇐. ARE YOU RELATED TO THE DECEASED?

MY UNCLE HE VAS. ONLY 45 YEARS, HE VAS. DRIVE THE BUS, HE DID. DROP DEAD, HE DID.

AND WHERE IS THE GRIEVING WIDOW?

IN THE KITCHEN, SHE IS. WHO YOU?

AH, I AM FROM THE ***OFFICE OF OPPORTUNITY.*** WE HEAR ABOUT THESE THINGS AND DO WHAT WE CAN. EXCUSE, PLEASE. ***MERCI!***

MAMMER --WHAT IS?
DON'T KNOW --SOME KIND OF DOOHICKUM...

"DOOHICKUM"? MADAME --THIS IS A HIGHLY SOPHISTICATED EDUCATIONAL TOOL! A DEMONSTRATION! YOU WISH TO KNOW YOUR SON'S INCOME IN FIVE YEARS SHOULD HE ENTER THE FIELD OF MEDICINE--

YOU SIMPLY PUNCH IN YOUR QUESTION... DO YOU READ INTERLAC?
NO ...

NEVER FEAR! WHEN YOU TRADE FOR THIS UNIT, OOO PROVIDES A NIGHT COURSE IN INTERLAC AT YOUR CONVENIENCE, OVER THE HOME COMPUTER, AT HOME!

YOU ARE ABSOLUTELY GUARANTEED MASTERY OF THIS SIMPLE DEVICE! IT'S EVERY CITIZEN'S RIGHT!
MADAME, YOUR CHILDREN'S FUTURE COULD VERY WELL DEPEND ON THIS VITAL CULTURAL INSTRUMENT. OOO WANTS YOU TO HAVE IT.
WHAT YOU DINK, HEY?
WE DUNT WANT DIE DUMB OR YOUNG! WE DUNT!
HOW MUCH IS COSTING?
I NOTICED A FINE PAIR OF PLATED CANDELABRA--WORTH, PERHAPS, A TENTH OF THE COMPUTER'S TRUE VALUE...
4

THE OFFICE DEMANDS A TOKEN PAYMENT, POLITICS. I'M SURE YOU UNDERSTAND.
FOR THE SAKE OF DAS CHILDREN.
WELL, WE ARE DENKING CHOO.
MY PLEASURE, MY PLEASURE. JUST FILL OUT YOUR NAME AND ADDRESS AND PUNCH IT IN... AN OOO REP WILL BE BY SHORTLY TO BEGIN INSTRUCTING YOU IN THE PROPER USE.
GENUINE PLATINUM STICKS, ALL RIGHT. I'LL GIVE YOU ₩2500 FOR 'EM.
MASON, THEY'RE WORTH FIVE TIMES THAT! ₩10,000.
3000.
8.

YEAH, I'VE BEEN FAT AND I'VE BEEN THIN...
LETRITIA, MY SUCCULENT EGG DEPOSITOR--WILT THOU JOIN ME FOR DIN DIN AT THE FRITZY RITZ?

WELL, ZONE, THIS IS A SURPRISE.
OPPORKNOCKITY HAS TUNED MY PIANO! ENTER!

PUT IT IN A SAFE SPOT, KID.
YOU BET!
5

DIDN'T YOU MAKE RESERVATIONS?
ALVIN K. JONES! LOOK AT THIS MOB! WE COULD STARVE TO DEATH BEFORE THEY SEAT US!
PFISTER PARTY OF FIVE, PLEASE... PFISTER PARTY OF FIVE...
5

I SHOULDN'T HAVE TO MAKE A RESERVATION! I AM AN ENTERTAINER ...AN ACTOR... SIR!
YES SIR, IF YOU'LL GIVE ME YOUR NAME ...
I'M DOCTOR CLONEZONE, WINNER OF THE NOBEL PRIZE IN MEDICINE... I WAS TOLD THERE WOULD BE A TABLE...
OF COURSE, IF YOU ARE UNABLE TO ACCOMODATE US...
OH! A DOCTOR! I'M SURE IT'S JUST A MIX-UP! ONE MOMENT, DR. CLONEZONE, SIR!

SHORTLY.
YASS...THE OLD "DOCTOR" ROUTINE USUALLY DOES THE TRICK!
CLONEZONE YOU'RE SUCH A CARD! HEH HEH HEH...

"SURE," THEY SAID. "HAVE A SEAT. ONLY, DON'T PASS OUT ON THE TABLE..."

DR. CLONEZONE, I HATE TO BOTHER YOU...
YASS ..?
6

WE HAVE AN EMERGENCY--OUR CHEF JUST COLLAPSED ON THE KITCHEN FLOOR --WILL YOU COME?

CHOKE!

CERTAINLY! DR. CLONEZONE IS EVER READY TO AID THOSE IN NEED.
THIS WAY, SIR.

THERE HE IS-- A HUMAN, AS YOU CAN SEE...
GREAT! I MINORED IN HUMAN PHYSIOLOGY! OKAY, ANY HISTORY OF HEART TROUBLE? STAND ASIDE, GIVE ME ROOM...

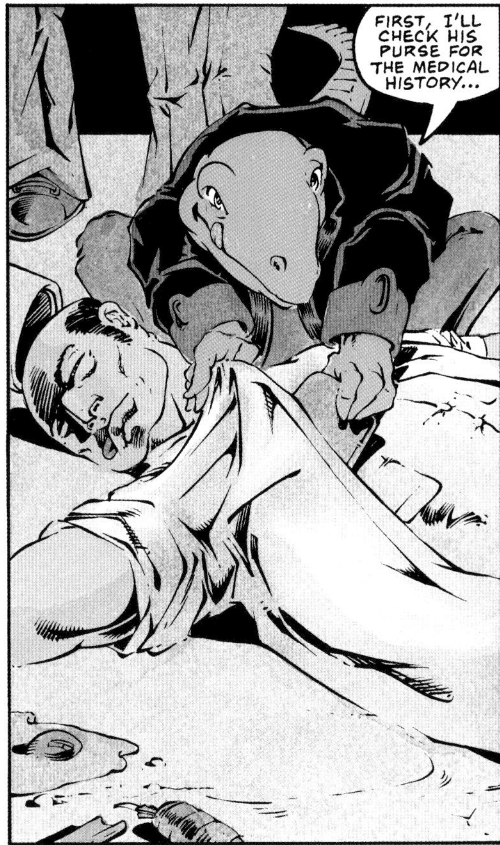
FIRST, I'LL CHECK HIS PURSE FOR THE MEDICAL HISTORY...

800...850... THIS GUY'S LOADED!

HOT WATER! ON THE DOUBLE! NOTHING IN THE PURSE...

SOMETIMES THEY KEEP THEIR MEDICAL INFO IN THE WRIST CHRONOMETER...
MORE PLATINUM, FROM THE LOOK OF IT...
7

WHERE'S THAT HOT WATER? A MAN'S LIFE IS AT STAKE!
BUT HE SAID ...

HE SAID HE VAS ...
A FEW DROPS ON THE CRANIUM...

FROM THE OFFICE OF OPPORTUNITY, HE VAS...

ZEN, SELL MY AUNT A HOME COMPUTER, HE DID...

GLEEP!

DR. CLONEZONE, COULD I SEE SOME IDENTIFICATION?

STEP ON IT, LETRITIA! THE OFFICE OF OPPORTUNITY IS CLOSING EARLY TONIGHT!
ZONE! I DIDN'T GET TO FINISH MY DESSERT!
END

NEXUS
S.RUDE 05

ALPH AND BETA?! NO... NO! LEAVE ME! PLEASE!
OH, NO, HORATIO... WE'VE COME TO FIX THINGS...
THAT'S RIGHT, HORATIO... THIS HAS GONE FAR ENOUGH... YOU AREN'T HEEDING THE DREAMS...
YOU ASKED FOR IT!
NEXUS®
RICK OLIVER EDITOR
STEVE HAYNIE LETTERS
LES DORSCHEID COLORS
ERIC SHANOWER INKS
STEVE RUDE PENCILS
MIKE BARON SCRIPT
I ask you to think on the hours when one sleeps. Do you know what happens then? The body may lie still in bed, but what happens to the thoughts —— the spirit? With what ancient demons does it spend its time? And in what deeds?
——Ardel Wray and Joseph Mischel, *Isle of the Dead*

I'M DREAMING NOW... YES! YOU ARE NOT REAL! THIS IS BUT A DREAM!
WE ARE HERE, HORATIO ...
AND WE ARE REAL.
LEAVE ME ALONE! OR I'LL KILL YOU! UNGH! UNGH!
BUT YOU ARE NOT KILLING, HORATIO... THAT IS THE PROBLEM...
FIZZLE...
FIZZZZT!
LOOK AT HOW YOU TREAT THE SACRED WATER...
DON'T PUT ME IN THERE, I BEG OF YOU!
WE KNOW WHAT THE PROBLEM IS...
BOSS
IT'S YOUR CONSCIENCE...
THAT'S RIGHT. SO WE'RE GOING TO FIX IT.
NO...

YOU MUST GET IN THE TANK NOW, HORATIO...
HELP ME, SOMEBODY! PLEASE!
YOU'LL THANK US FOR THIS SOMEDAY, HORATIO...
NO!
NO!
SPLOOSH
GLUB!
HE'S PANICKING... HE HAS FORGOTTEN HOW TO BREATHE IN THE TANK.
THEN TAKE MY HAND, BROTHER...
AND LET US BEGIN.
3

OUTSIDE NEXUS' QUARTERS.
HELLO, KREED. ANY SIGN OF NEXUS?
HELLO, MEZZ. NOT A SIGN. THE DOOR HAS NOT OPENED IN FIVE CYCLES.
I'LL GIVE YOU 500 FOR THAT STUPID LITTLE ASHTRAY.
I THOUGHT HE'D LIKE TO KNOW--SUNDRA IS LEAVING.
YOU MUST BE STUPID TO MAKE SUCH AN OFFER. THIS IS AN AUTHENTIC YLUM ARTIFACT.

HE SEEKS PRIVACY AND HE SHALL HAVE IT.
THAT DOOR KIND OF MAKES YOU SUPERFLUOUS, HUH?
I LIVE TO SERVE GREAT NEXUS. WITHOUT HIS LIGHT, MY LIFE HAS NO MEANING.
ALMOST HAD 'IM.
YOWZAH.
SWOG. IF HE COMES OUT, TELL HIM ABOUT SUNDRA.

WHAT FUNCTION DOES THE BOY SERVE?
ONE OF NEXUS' PERSONAL CHOICES. AN ORPHAN. NEXUS PULLED HIM OFF THE WRECKAGE ON ZEFFERILLI.
I, TOO, WOULD LEARN FROM THE GREAT ONE. IF ONLY I COULD SEE HIM.
PATIENCE, BROTHER TWILLY. HE HAS NEVER BEEN ALONE THIS LONG BEFORE...

COME ON, TWILLY. HE'S NOT COMING OUT TODAY. LET US TRADE THE SECRETS OF DEATH.
LEAD ON, BROTHER KREED.
4

SHOULD ANYONE BUT ME ATTEMPT TO MANIPULATE THESE LOCKS, THEY WOULD LEARN MY SECRETS THE HARD WAY.
KLIK
KLIK
KLIK
KLIK
KLIK
KLIK
KLIK
I'M NOT LOOKING.
HERE, IN MY ARMORARIUM, I KEEP ALIVE THE SECRET WAYS OF DEATH. I SALVAGE AND RESTORE THE ANCIENT WEAPONS. REVOLVERS. KNIVES. NEUTRON BOMBS.
QUITE A COLLECTION. AND NO ONE KNOWS OF THIS...
BUT ME AND THEE.
KICK ME
MISSILE
YOUR DEATH, BROTHER, TO SPILL THE BEANS.
KREED IS GENEROUS WITH TWILLY.
NOW TWILLY HAS SOMETHING FOR KREED.
A SMART BULLET.
TAKE THE MONOCLE.
MIRABLE DICTU! I SEE FROM THE BULLET!
YES--IT'S THOUGHT ACTIVATED. YOU HAVE A FEEL FOR THIS SORT OF THING...
MMMMMMMMM
MAGNIFICO! I MUST HAVE MORE!
SWOOOOOOOOOOO
IT WILL KILL WITH A THRUST, LIKE A BULLET, AND RETURN TO YOU--WITH PROPER TRAINING.
WHOOOO
5

I AM RIGHT TO TRUST YOU. WE WILL GO KILLING TOGETHER.
ZIPPPF
WHO ARE YOU, KREED? WHERE DO YOU COME FROM?
I AM A QUATRO. I WAS RAISED BY GUCCI MONKS TO BE THE ULTIMATE ASSASSIN. I KILL AS EASILY AS MOST PEOPLE BREATHE, AND WITH AS LITTLE THOUGHT. I HAVE KILLED 2718 SENTIENT BEINGS, MANY OF MY OWN RACE. BUT ALWAYS, THESE WERE PETTY KILLINGS. MOTIVATED BY GREED, HATRED, OR ENVY.
AND THEN ONE DAY, I HAD HAD ENOUGH. ALL DRIVE LEFT ME. I WAS USELESS. THE GUCCI MONKS CAST ME OUT. I WANDERED, BEREFT OF VISION.
IT WAS A BAD TIME FOR ME. I WAS ON PLUTO WHEN I FIRST LEARNED OF NEXUS... HOW HE KILLED. WHY HE KILLED. FOR HE HAD WHAT I LACKED--A REASON.
TELE TRACK
BLACK HOLE
MY FAITH WAS REKINDLED.
I FOUND YLUM. AND HERE I WAIT, AND SERVE, AND LEARN. AND WHEN GREAT NEXUS NEXT EMERGES, I WILL ACCOMPANY HIM AND LEARN OF HIS PURPOSE.
AND YOU, TWILLY. WHAT BRINGS YOU TO THIS ASYLUM OF DEATH?
I, TOO, SEEK THE GREAT ONE'S WISDOM.
I KNEW IT. WHEN NEXUS EMERGES, WE BOTH WILL GO WITH HIM ON AN ODDYSSEY OF DEATH THAT WILL BE LONG REMEMBERED.
SUCH IS MY DREAM.
6

PACKED INTO ONE MAMMOTH DEEP SPACE CRUISER, S&J ENTERPRISES BEGINS ITS JOURNEY TO THE CENTER OF THE WEB, AN INTERSTELLAR ASSOCIATION WITH ITS ORIGINS ON EARTH.
SUNDRA, MR. EL DOAUD IS STANDING BY.
MR. EL DOAUD? SUNDRA PEALE. HOW MAY I HELP YOU?
I WISH TO COMMISSION A SOLAR YACHT CAPABLE OF A NINE ASTRONOMICAL UNIT RANGE, AND CAN SLEEP SIX.
I THINK WE CAN ACCOMODATE YOU, BUT THERE IS A WAITING LIST.
I MUST HAVE IT BY FEBRUARY 28, EARTHSIDE, IN ORDER TO QUALIFY FOR THE EARTH-MOON REGATTA!
EVERYBODY SAYS THE SAME THING. WE'LL SEE WHAT WE CAN DO, MR. EL DOAUD.

THAT'S RIGHT--THEY RELOCATED TO SARED-JYN AND THEY'VE BEEN GUNNING FOR THE WEB EVER SINCE. BUT HERE'S THE HEAVY MOLECULE--THE WEB CLAIMS THAT THE GRAVITY WELL IS SAFE, TOO FAR FROM THE WEB TO AFFECT INHABITED SYSTEMS.

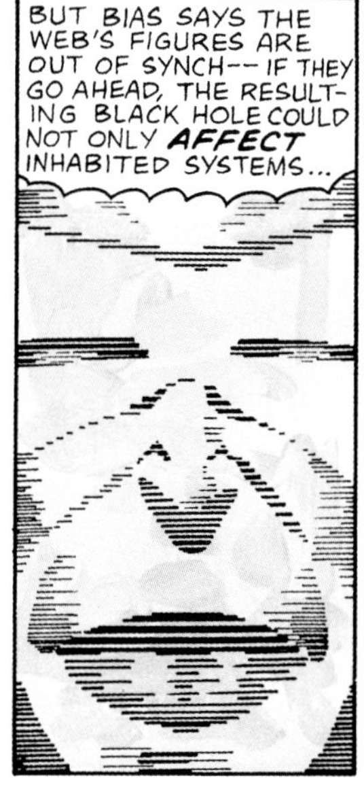
BUT BIAS SAYS THE WEB'S FIGURES ARE OUT OF SYNCH--IF THEY GO AHEAD, THE RESULTING BLACK HOLE COULD NOT ONLY AFFECT INHABITED SYSTEMS...

IT COULD SWALLOW OUR ENTIRE SOLAR SYSTEM. INCLUDING MARS.
WHEN DO THEY PLAN TO IMPLEMENT THIS PROJECT?

WITHIN THREE EARTH YEARS. BATTLE LINES ARE ALREADY BEING DRAWN. BELIEVE ME, SOME SYSTEMS ARE WILLING TO GO TO WAR OVER THIS. MARS TRIED FIGHTING IT FROM WITHIN CONGRESS. NOW THEY'RE TALKING ABOUT SECEDING FROM THE WEB.

THANK YOU, MARS. WE'LL REVIEW THE SITUATION MORE FULLY WHEN WE ARRIVE.

THIS SOUNDS LIKE SOMETHING THAT FAT FOOL OF A PRESIDENT WOULD TRY. HIM AND URSULA. GODDAMN THEM BOTH TO HELL.

ATLANTA, CAPITAL OF THE WEB.
AMBASSADOR IMADA, SIR.
AH, MADAME AMBASSADOR. HOW WAS YOUR MEETING WITH THE MARTIAN PRIME MINISTER?
AN UNQUALIFIED DISASTER.
IT IS TIME TO DROP THE PRETENSE. EVERY GOVERNMENT IN THE WEB KNOWS I AM YOUR SPY. THE ONLY PLACE THEY TREAT ME LIKE AN AMBASSADOR IS HERE.
YES. TOO BAD ABOUT THAT BIAS REPORT--I WONDER HOW THEY FOUND OUT?
8

I HAVE AN IDEA WHO MIGHT HAVE TOLD THEM. IT IS NOT IMPORTANT. I WILL GO TO ALPHA CENTAURI NEXT...
NO. I'M CANCELLING THAT PROGRAM. MARS IS MOVING TOWARD SECESSION. I WANT YOU TO GO TO MARS AND ARRANGE A TRANSFER OF POWER INTO FRIENDLIER HANDS.
IT IS NOT SAFE FOR ME ON MARS.
BLAST IT, COMMANDER-- YOU'RE THE ONLY ONE WHO CAN PULL THIS OFF. YOU AND BRANCH CORPS.
THE KID GLOVES ARE OFF! WE TRIED DIPLOMACY BY NORMAL CHANNELS.
IF MARS SECEDES, JUPITER WILL FOLLOW! AND ALPHA CENTAURI!
THE ONLY THING HOLDING THE WEB TOGETHER IS THE HOPE WE CAN DELIVER ON OUR ENERGY FUTURES.
NOW MARS IS YOUR NUMBER ONE PRIORITY. END OF DISCUSSION.
MR. PRESIDENT --
IS THERE ANY TRUTH TO THE RUMOR THAT YOU TRIED SQUEEZING HOLES IN ROSS 128 SECTOR...AND THERE WAS AN... ACCIDENT?
MY GOD. WELL, THAT'S WHY YOU'RE HEAD OF BRANCH CORPS. HOW MUCH DO YOU KNOW?
IT SUCKED IN A PLANET NAMED PERIWINKLE --500,000 DEAD.
IT WAS A STUPID, AVOIDABLE TRAGEDY. THOSE RESPONSIBLE WENT INTO THE HOLE. BELIEVE ME, WE'VE CHECKED GRAVITY WELL FROM EVERY ANGLE. IT'S SAFE. IT MUST WORK, OR CIVILIZATION COULD SLIDE INTO A FRIGHTENING DARK AGE.
CIVILIZATION-- WARM FOOD, COMFORTABLE SHELTER, THE ARTS--EVERYTHING THAT MAKES LIFE WORTHWHILE--ALL DEPENDS ON ENERGY.
I'VE HAD TO MAKE SOME HARD CHOICES LATELY--BUT HISTORY WILL ABSOLVE ME. YOU HAVE YOUR INSTRUCTIONS.
VERY GOOD, MR. PRESIDENT.

POMPOUS JACKASS... HE HAS PLACED ALL THE WEB'S EGGS IN ONE BASKET.
AND I DO NOT THINK THE BASKET WILL HOLD THEM.
MADAME, WE ARE LANDING.
THANK YOU, MAURICE.
CASTLE IMADA-- LOCATED ON A LONELY CRAG IN THE NORTH ATLANTIC.
WELCOME HOME, MADAME.
THANK YOU, DEREK. PLEASE CALL A GENERAL MEETING FOR NINE P.M. AND TUCK IN YOUR SHIRT.
The Nursery
N
SHEENA! SCARLET!
MOMMY! MOMMY!
MOMMY! MOMMY!
MMMMM. GIVE MOMMY A BIG KISS.
I CAN READ! BUT SHEENA CAN'T!
CAN TOO! I JUST CAN'T READ ENGLISH!
10

9:05 P.M.

IF THE WEB PURSUES THIS POLICY, I BELIEVE THE ENTIRE SOLAR SYSTEM, AS WELL AS ALPHA CENTAURI, WILL BE DESTROYED.

THOSE WHO ELECT TO STAY WITH CASTLE IMADA WILL FIND FULL SECURITY ON PROCYON. YOUR FAMILIES WILL BE TRANSPORTED. YOUR NEEDS WILL BE PROVIDED. THERE IS NO RUSH. BUT I ADVISE YOU ALL TO ACT ECONOMICALLY.

11

A HALF CYCLE HAS PASSED SINCE ALPH AND BETA PUT NEXUS IN THE TANK.
HE'S READY.
LET'S BRING HIM OUT.

HIS HEAD IS HEALED. THE TANK HAS SET HIM RIGHT. NOW WE MUST GO TO WORK ON HIS BODY.

OHHH...
I MUST HAVE FALLEN ASLEEP.. WHAT A DREAM... WHAT A NIGHTMARE ...

ASLEEP?!

GOOD MORNING, HORATIO.
ALPH!
I'M BETA.

I'M ALPH. HOW ARE YOU FEELING?
I AM STILL ASLEEP. I AM TRAPPED IN THIS NIGHT-MARE.
YOU HAVE LET YOURSELF SLIDE, HORATIO. YOU HAVE BECOME A BLUNTED BLADE.
THE TIME HAS COME TO GRIND A NEW EDGE.
12

WHAT WOULD YOU HAVE ME DO?
YOU HAVE TO GET IN SHAPE.
SO YOU CAN SEEK OUT THE MURDERERS AMONG US.
THEY NEED TO DIE. AND ONLY YOU CAN KILL THEM. DO YOU SEE THAT NOW?
YESS...
THEN YOU MUST BEGIN WITH THE WEIGHTS.
AND SO THE TRAINING BEGINS, SUPERVISED BY ALPH AND BETA.
KEEP YOUR KNEES LOCKED! BOUNCE ON THE BALLS OF YOUR FEET!
ONE MORE KILOMETER! YOU CAN DO IT!
GASP!

ON THE FOURTH DAY.
COME WITH US, HORATIO. WE WANT TO SHOW YOU SOMETHING.
ALL RIGHT.
SOON, IN THE RUINS.
GO INTO THAT ROOM, HORATIO.
WHY? IT SCARES ME.
YOU **MUST**, HORATIO.
THERE IS SOMETHING IN HERE WITH ME.
ALPH?
BETA?
YOU! I **KILLED** YOU!
YOU **MISSED!** NOW IT'S **MY** TURN!

DIE!
AHHHH!

ZOW
NOOO!
DIE!
ZOW
ZOW

CRAWL!
CRAWL AND I'LL END IT!
NOOO!

NOOO!
ZOW
ZOW

THEN DIE SLOWLY!

NO!
15

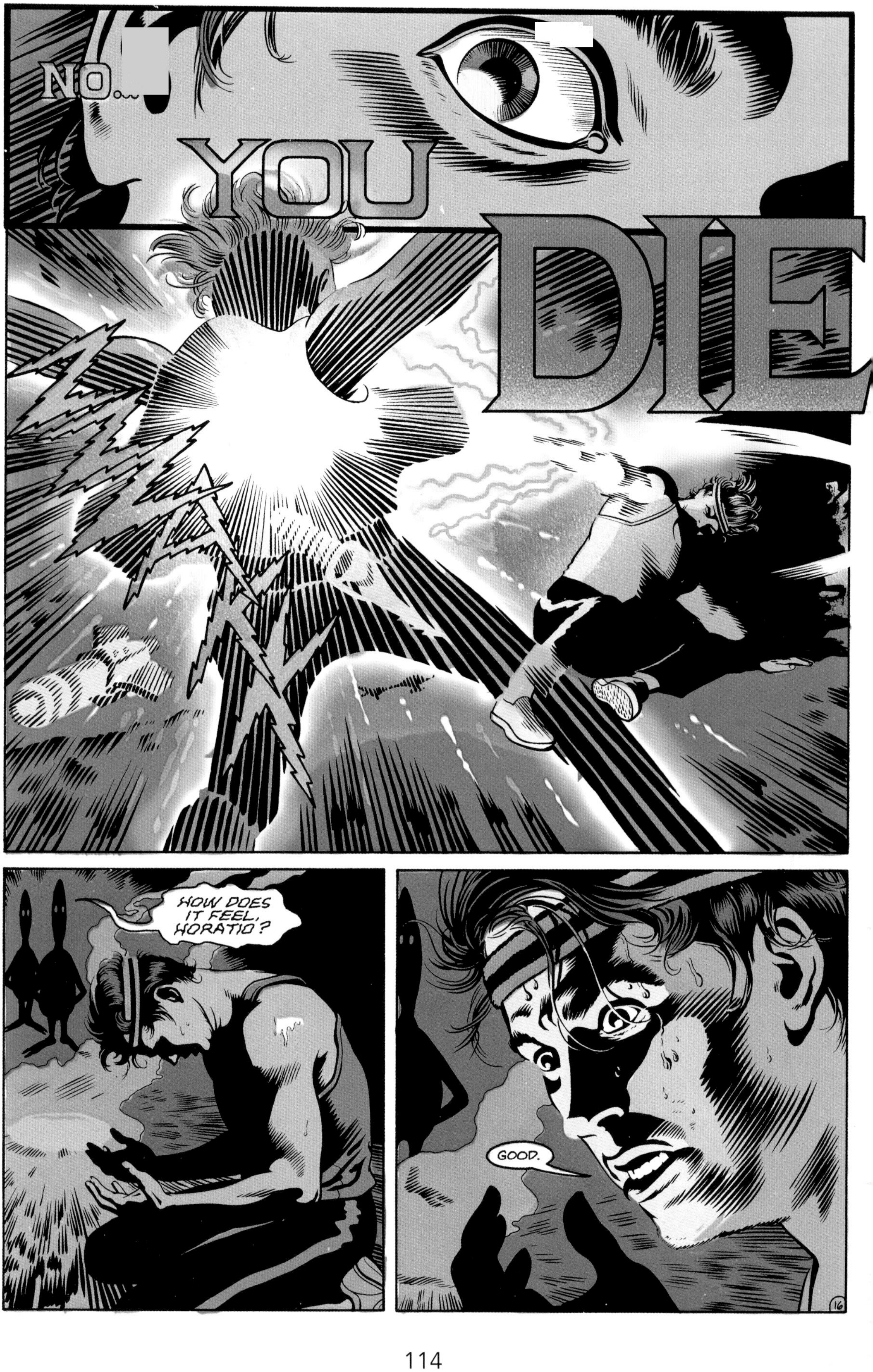

NO...

YOU

DIE

MARS--NEW HOME OF S&J SOLAR SAILCRAFT.
SUNDRA, THE MILLERS ARE HERE.
GREAT. WE DON'T HAVE THE MILLING ROOM SET UP YET. HAVE THEM EXPLAIN THE INSTALLATION TO JIL --IN THE MEANTIME, THEY CAN UNLOAD IN WAREHOUSE #3.
EXCUSE ME, WE'RE LOOKING FOR OUR DAUGHTER, SUNDRA PEALE...
THERE SHE IS!
HOW'S MY LITTLE GIRL?
GREAT! IT'S GOOD TO BE BACK.
THIS IS YOUR HOME, DEAR. I ALWAYS KNEW YOU'D RETURN SOMEDAY.
OF COURSE YOU'LL BE LIVING AT HOME.
NOPE, I'VE GOT AN APARTMENT HERE.
BUT BABY, WE HAVE YOUR OLD ROOM SET UP AND EVERYTHING...
HA HA! SOME THINGS NEVER CHANGE!
YOUR FATHER AND I WERE HOPING WE COULD ALL BE TOGETHER AGAIN.
WE ARE ALL TOGETHER AGAIN! BUT NOT ALL THE TIME. NOW I WANT YOU BOTH TO PRETEND THAT I'M AN ADULT, THAT I CAN TAKE CARE OF MYSELF, AND EVEN THAT I HAVE A PURPOSE IN LIFE OUTSIDE YOUR HAPPY HOME.
BUT YOU'LL ALWAYS BE OUR LITTLE GIRL TO YOUR FATHER AND ME... ARE YOU EATING WELL?
THAT'S WHY I'M NOT LIVING AT HOME!
DARNED IMPRESSIVE. WHO REALLY OWNS THIS OPERATION?

EEEEE
REAAAAHH
YLUM--SIX CYCLES HAVE PASSED SINCE NEXUS WAS LAST SEEN.
WHAT IS HAPPENING? WHY ARE THEY DOING THIS?
ZOK ZOK ZOK
REEEEEEKKK
IT MEANS HE HAS BEGUN TO DREAM. AND THE DREAM IS POWERFUL.
I CAN'T STAND IT ANYMORE!
BAM BAM
CEASE! IF YOU WANT TO DIE, I WILL HELP YOU. BUT DO NOT MARK THE MASTER'S DOOR WITH YOUR BLOOD.
YES! YES! HELP ME DIE, KREED! LIFE IS TOO MUCH HURT!
THINK WHAT YOU ARE SAYING. I DO NOT JUDGE AND I WILL HELP YOU.
HELP ME DIE.
STOP!
LET HIM GO.
DO NOT INTERFERE, TYRONE.
IF THE CITIZEN TRULY WISHES TO DESTROY HIMSELF, LET HIM DO IT ELSEWHERE. THIS IS A PUBLIC THOROUGHFARE.
IT IS THE DOMAIN OF NEXUS.
18

BEYOND THAT DOOR LIES THE DOMAIN OF NEXUS.

OUT HERE IS A COMMUNITY.

THERE ARE CHILDREN PLAYING. THIS IS NOT A PLACE FOR DEATH. AND IF THEY WISH TO DIE SO BADLY, DO NOT ASSIST THEM. ANYONE WHO CANNOT DO IT FOR THEMSELVES DOES NOT TRULY WISH TO DIE.

LET'S GO GET THAT HEAD LOOKED AT CITIZEN.
WHY DID YOU INTERFERE?
HMMM...

PERHAPS TYRONE IS RIGHT. AT LEAST HE SEEMS TO HAVE A PURPOSE.
CRACK
UNLIKE US, I SUPPOSE.

DO YOU SEEK PURPOSE?
19

THEN FOLLOW ME TO EARTH! THERE ARE MURDERERS FOR ALL BRAVE ENOUGH TO JOIN ME!
AT LAST!
NEXT MONTH:
INTO THE WEB!

CLONEZONE THE HILARIATOR

THE JOKE DOCTOR

MIKE BARON STORY · MARK A. NELSON ART

LES DORSCHEID COLORS · STEVE HAYNIE LETTERS · RICK OLIVER EDITS

DOC--YOU SAW. TELL ME-- WHERE DID I GO WRONG? HOW DID I LOSE THEM?

WELL...

THIS TIME, HONESTLY, YOU WEREN'T SO FUNNY.

GOSH, THANKS!

BUT SERIOUSLY, DOC! I'VE USED THE SAME EXACT JOKES AND ***KILLED***. BUT LAST NIGHT, I COULD HAVE BEEN TALKING TO THE TABLES.

WELL, WHEN WE KNOW WHY WE ARE FUNNY SOME NIGHTS, AND WHY WE DIE ON OTHERS, THEN WE KNOW THE SECRET OF HUMOR, AND BY EXTENSION, THE VERY SECRET TO THE MYSTERY OF LIFE...

THANKS AGAIN, DOC! THE METER IS RUNNING!

DOCTOR OF JOKOLOGY
HILARITUS EMERITUS
HA HA
ZONE, WHAT WE HAVE HERE IS A LOG JAM SITUATION. SOMETIMES A SINGLE LOG IS ALL THAT IS NECESSARY TO JAR IT LOOSE. YOU HAVE A CLASSIC SITUATION-- ALL YOU ARE LACKING IS THE KEY LOG.
THAT'S THE BUNK, DOC. THE MATERIAL WAS WRONG.
DIR
VANCE
WHAT YOU NEED IS A SURE-FIRE GAG.
NOW YOU'RE TALKING! A JOKE THAT CAN'T FAIL TO GET LAUGHS!
I MAY HAVE JUST THE THING... AH... HMM... NO... AH, HERE WE ARE!
GAK!
WAH--! BOO HOO HOO!
YOU DON'T THINK THIS IS FUNNY?
NICE KNOWIN' YOU, DOC ...
WAIT--IT WAS A JOKE, CLONEZONE.
THAT'S WHAT SCARES ME.
3

MUCH LATER...

SO THAT'S THE JOKE. YOU DON'T THINK IT'S FUNNY?

DOC, I AM IN DEEP, DEEP TROUBLE. AND SO ARE YOU. IF I DON'T BUST LOOSE SOME YOKS TONIGHT, I DON'T GET PAID.

VANCE

WELL, I'M HERE IF YOU NEED TO TALK.

THAT'S STRONG COMFORT, DOC.

WELL, GOOD LUCK!

GLEEP!

OH YES-- I MEAN, DROP DEAD!

4

ZONE--YOU ON STRICT PROBATION, MAN! THE FAT GUY SAYS--KILL OR BE KILLED!
COMEDY CLUB
OKAY, TOO-TALL! OKAY! SOMETIMES I WONDER WHOSE SIDE YOU'RE ON! ALVIN! I GOTTA RELAX!

I WAS THE ONE TALKED THE FAT GUY INTO PUTTING YOU ON FOR A WEEK--SO HE CUT YOU BACK TO OPENING FOR THE GREAT GLIGNITCH--SO GO OUT THERE AND KILL!
HAND ME THAT CREAM BASE, WILLYA? WHAT'S THE HOUSE LIKE? ANY HUMANS?
A COUPLE.

BASICALLY, YOU GOT A LOT OF CRUSTACEOUS TYPES FROM TAU CETI--HARD TO AMUSE AND LOUSY TIPPERS...
OH, SWELL!

PLUS WHICH YOU GOT YOUR MERCUREAN STONE CRITTERS...
STONE CRITTERS!

PLUS WHICH, ONE TABLE ASSORTED MEAN DRUNKS CLOSE TO THE STAGE.
ALVIN, ALVIN! TOO-TALL--YOU GOT A BLASTER YOU CAN LOAN ME?

SORRY, MAN. LEFT MINE AT HOME.

FIVE MINUTES, ZONE!
I HOPE I HAVE A NICE FUNERAL.

OFFICIAL SCHAPP SCAVENGER? THE PRESIDENT. NO OFFICIAL FLOWER, BUT THE NATIONAL SCENT IS *TUNA*.

GRR-- GRUMBLE MUMBLE

O--*KAY!* NO SLUR INTENDED AGAINST THE FINE GOVERNMENT...

YOUR INDULGENCE ONE MOMENT, ESTEEMED AND ERUDITE THINKING BEINGS...

TA-DA!

GOT CAUGHT IN A BLACK HOLE TIME WARP! JUST BLEW IN FROM THE LITTLE BIG HORN!

YOU CALL THIS HUMOR? PTUI! I KNOW WHAT HUMOR IS! I AM NOT STUPID!

NO, OF COURSE NOT, SIR! UH, UH, SO GOD'S CREATING THE UNIVERSE AND HE WANTS TO GET IT ON VID, RIGHT? SO HE PUTS MICHAEL, HIS RIGHT HAND GUY, OUT ON A SKYHOOK...

THREE MINUTES LATER.
...SO HE HITS THE NEUTRON WITH THE IVORY POOL CUE, NICE BANKSHOT OFF A ROCK, BAM! IT HITS THE HYDROGEN CLOUD AND BEFORE YOU KNOW IT --POW! SUPER-NOVA!
FIREWORKS! COMETS! CARBON IS FORMING AND IT'S ALL HAPPENING! WHAT A SHOW!

BANG! BASH! CRASH! IT ALL HAPPENS! PLASMA IS FORMING! GOD TURNS TO MICHAEL! "YOU GOT IT?" HE SHOUTS.

MICHAEL MAKES A BIG THUMBS UP-- "READY WHEN YOU ARE, BIG GUY!"

HOO-HOO-HOO...

HOO HOO HOO! HA HA! HA HA HA! HA HA HA HA! HOO HOO!
7

AH HA HA! HOO HOO!
HE IS FUNNY...
HEH HEH...
THAT'S A RELIEF, PAL! FOR A SECOND, YOU LOOKED LIKE YOU WANTED TO TURN ME INTO AN OVERNIGHT BAG.
HEY YOU STONIES! YOU GUYS ARE REALLY SOMETHING ELSE... STATUESQUE! WHADDAYA SHAVE WITH? PNEUMATICS AND A #9 COLD CHISEL, RIGHT? I HEAR YOU GUYS SAVE THE CHIPS FOR DRIVEWAYS!
HA HA HO HO HEE HEE
AND SO...
THE TAX FORM CONTAINS SOMETHING NEW THIS YEAR-- AN ENEMA, A BLOOD TAP, AND AN AUTOSEX TAB...
YOU JUST DRAIN YOUR BLOOD, GIVE YOURSELF AN ENEMA AND ☆◎✪# YOURSELF --SAVE THE GOVERNMENT THE TROUBLE...
HA HA HOO HOO HEH HEH HEH HEH HEE HEE
HA HA HA HA HEE HEE HEE
HO HO HO HA HA HA HEE HEE HA HO
HOO HOO HOO HA HA HA!
NEXT DAY.
DOC--THE JOKE WORKED! YOU'RE A GENIUS!
THANKS.
END

S.RUDE '85

ATLANTA
THE PRESIDENT OF THE WEB CROUCHES IN THE CENTER OF HIS VAST AND FRAGILE CONSTRUCT.
HE'S WEB BOUND, MR. PRESIDENT. NO DOUBT ABOUT IT.
I WANT A FULL SCALE ALERT. I DON'T WANT HIM PAST PLUTO.
MR. PRESIDENT, THERE ARE AT LEAST 850,000 POSSIBLE TARGETS WITHIN THE WEB. MAYBE YOU'RE OVERREACTING.

A FULL SCALE ALERT! DO YOU HEAR ME? GENERAL?
YES, SIR.
NEXUS IS A FUGITIVE IN THE WEB. WE HAVE TO APPREHEND HIM.

TOP SECRET, GENERAL.
OF COURSE.

WE DON'T WANT RUMORS CIRCULATING THAT THE PRESIDENT IS A MASS MURDERER!
DAMN IT, HUBERT! SQUEEZING THOSE SINGULARITIES TOGETHER WAS A CALCULATED RISK.
THE CALCULATIONS WERE OFF, APPARENTLY.
THE ENERGY SECRETARY ASSURED ME THAT ORTON SYSTEM WAS IN NO DANGER! HE GOT SUCKED INTO THE HOLE LEAVING ME HOLDING THE BAG! THE WEB IS FALLING APART... AND NOW THIS!
HAVE YOU LOCATED IMADA YET?
NO, SIR. WE DISPATCHED A JET --THEY SHOULD BE LANDING AT ANY MINUTE.

CASTLE IMADA IN THE NORTH ATLANTIC.
IT'S THE DARNDEST THING, MR. PRESIDENT. THE PLACE IS DESERTED. LIKE THEY CLEARED OUT.
CLEARED OUT? THAT'S PREPOSTEROUS!
YES, SIR. THERE'S NOTHING HERE BUT THE FURNITURE AND SOME OLD, OBSOLETE WEAPONS.
IMADA HAS CUT AND RUN! I'M ALL ALONE!
PLEASE, SIR. GET HOLD OF YOURSELF! YOU CAN OVERCOME THESE DIFFICULTIES!
TIME! I NEED MORE TIME! MY ENEMIES HAVE PUT HIM UP TO THIS...
MR. PRESIDENT, EVEN IF, BY SOME FREAK CHANCE, HE IS AFTER YOU, WE CAN PROTECT YOU.
HE'S JUST A SINGLE BEING!
29TH WEB FLEET, IN ORBIT ABOVE PLUTO.
ATTENTION ALL CRAFT-- THIS IS FLEET COMMANDER JONES. MOVE TO ORANGE ALERT-- PREPARE TO INTERCEPT SMALL VESSEL ON COURSE TO EARTH.
HOW DO THEY EXPECT US TO SPOT ONE SHIP? IT'S ABSURD.
OH NO? TAKE A LOOK AT THE SCREEN --THAT THING'S THROWING OFF RADIATION LIKE A QUASAR!
HOLY --!

NEXUS®
INTO THE WEB
WRITER BARON
ARTIST RUDE
ATTENTION NEXUS! IF YOU PROCEED YOU WILL BE OBLITERATED! TURN BACK NOW!
GREAT NEXUS MAKES NO SECRET OF HIS MISSION... A TELEPATHIC COMMUNICATION TO THE WEB... THE INELUCTABLE MARCH OF HISTORY...
HOW DID THEY KNOW TO EXPECT US?
Homer was wrong in saying: "Would that strife might perish from among gods and men!" He did not see that he was praying for the destruction of the universe; for, if his prayer were heard, all things would pass away.
–Heraclitus

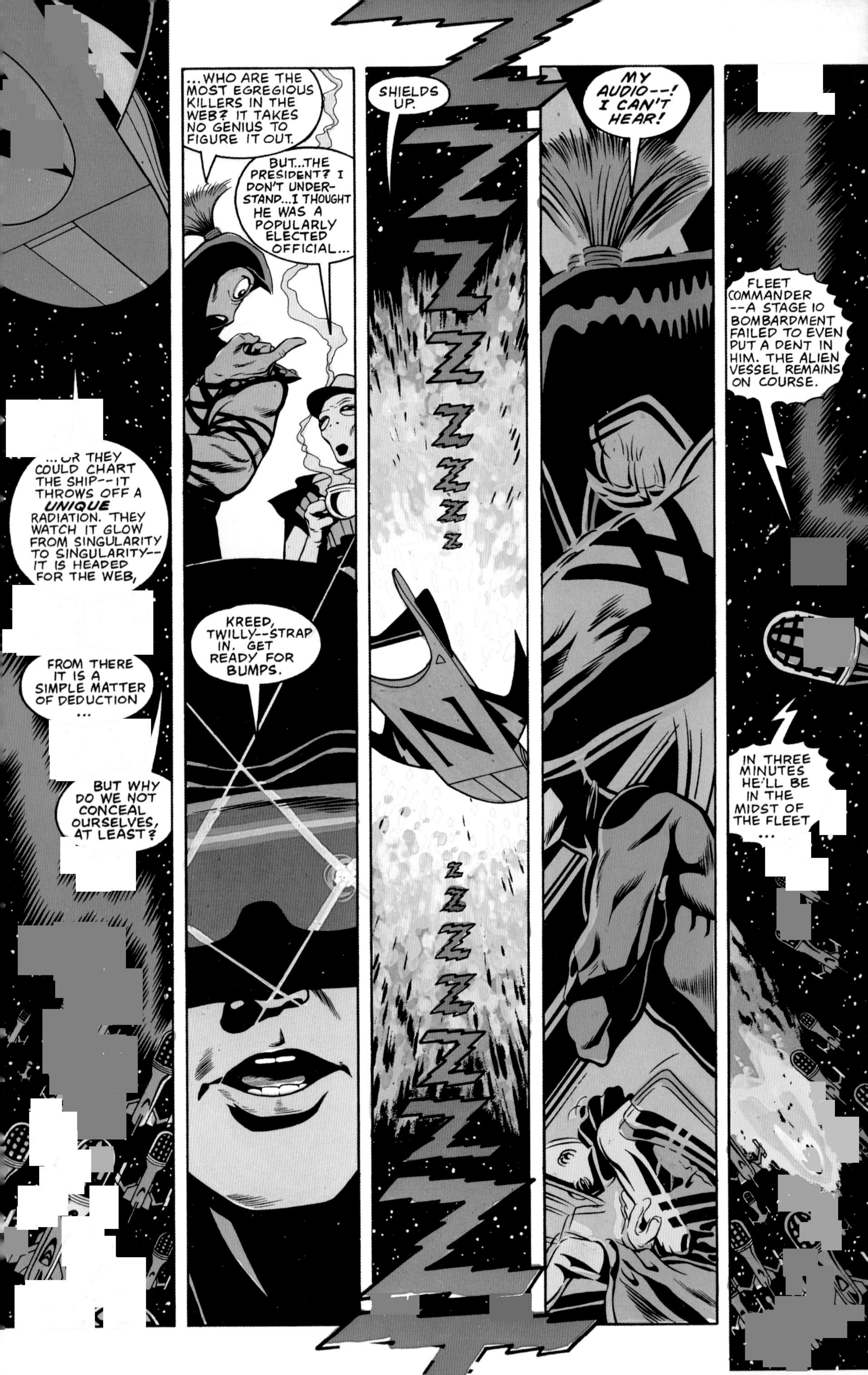
...OR THEY COULD CHART THE SHIP--IT THROWS OFF A UNIQUE RADIATION. THEY WATCH IT GLOW FROM SINGULARITY TO SINGULARITY--IT IS HEADED FOR THE WEB,
FROM THERE IT IS A SIMPLE MATTER OF DEDUCTION ...
BUT WHY DO WE NOT CONCEAL OURSELVES, AT LEAST?
...WHO ARE THE MOST EGREGIOUS KILLERS IN THE WEB? IT TAKES NO GENIUS TO FIGURE IT OUT.
BUT...THE PRESIDENT? I DON'T UNDERSTAND...I THOUGHT HE WAS A POPULARLY ELECTED OFFICIAL...
KREED, TWILLY--STRAP IN. GET READY FOR BUMPS.
SHIELDS UP.
ZZZZZz
zzZZZZZ
MY AUDIO--! I CAN'T HEAR!
FLEET COMMANDER --A STAGE 10 BOMBARDMENT FAILED TO EVEN PUT A DENT IN HIM. THE ALIEN VESSEL REMAINS ON COURSE.
IN THREE MINUTES HE'LL BE IN THE MIDST OF THE FLEET ...

WE CAN'T OPEN FIRE OR WE'LL BE RISKING OUR OWN CRAFT. NOTIFY THE PRESIDENT--NEXUS HAS BROKEN THROUGH THE SPHERE OF PLUTO.
HIS CRAFT IS UTTERLY IMPERVIOUS TO OUR MOST POWERFUL WEAPONS. HE IS TRAILING A PLUME OF PLASMA FROM THE ION BOMBARDMENT.
THE CAPITAL WAR ROOM.
MR. PRESIDENT...?
I HEARD! DO YOU THINK I'M DEAF AND BLIND?!
SIR, IF YOU REMAIN ON EARTH THERE IS A STRONG LIKLIHOOD OF MASSIVE CIVILIAN CASUALTIES!
OH NO, HUBERT--THAT'S WHERE YOU'RE WRONG! IF WE'RE TO BELIEVE WHAT WE HEAR ABOUT NEXUS, HE'LL TURN BACK RATHER THAN RISK CIVILIAN CASUALTIES!
THAT'S ENOUGH! I WANT A COMPLETE NEWS BLACK-OUT ON THIS! NO ONE IS TO KNOW!
SIR, THE CHANCES ARE NIL THAT NEXUS WILL QUIT BEFORE YOU ARE DEAD. YOU YOURSELF VIEWED THOSE VIDS FROM ROSARIO...
LASER-DEFENSE
CLASSIFIED
5

MR. PRESIDENT, I'M AFRAID IT'S TOO LATE FOR THAT. I DON'T WANT TO ALARM YOU, BUT WE HAVE TO CONSIDER AN INCREASED ASSASSINATION THREAT...
THERE ARE THOSE WHO WILL SEE A SACRIFICE PLAY AS THE ONLY MEANS TO FORESTALL WHOLESALE SLAUGHTER...
I SEE...YES, THERE ARE SUCH PEOPLE...
CHERNENKO.
COMRADES, AS INCREDIBLE AS IT SEEMS, NEXUS IS GOING AFTER PRESIDENT OGLETHORP. WHAT AN OPPORTUNITY!
SOMEHOW, WE MUST PREVENT TWILLY FROM KILLING NEXUS UNTIL NEXUS KILLS OGLETHORP.
NATASHA, KONNIE, WE HAVE A PROBLEM. TWILLY IS VIRTUALLY INCOMMUNICADO.
WE CAN'T LOSE. WE ARE ASSURED OF NEXUS' DEATH.
BE NICE IF HE KILLS OGLETHORP FIRST, THOUGH, YAH?
LET'S JUST HOPE TWILLY REALIZES THE SITUATION. HOW GOES THE SEARCH FOR A MEANS TO DESTROY TWILLY?
STILL WORKING ON IT.
IT IS TIME TO CHOOSE GENERAL KROGH'S REPLACEMENT.
SEND IN THE APPLICANTS.
GREETINGS, EXALTED MEMBERS OF THE CENTRAL COMMITTEE. GENERALISSIMO SHUVELOF TUBUFFALO AT YOUR SERVICE.
LUCINDA DRAGONOVICH.
JOHANNIS HAGMAN.

GREAT ONE--THEY ARE ARRAYED BEFORE US ACROSS THE SPHERE OF SATURN. LET US TAKE EVASIVE ACTION!
LET THEM GET OUT OF THE WAY.
BUT GREAT ONE--WILL YOU PERMIT THEM TO STRIKE YOUR SHIP? LET US SHOW THEM OUR SKILL!
YES! LET FLY, "GREAT ONE!" ONE BOLT OF FUSION FROM YOUR HANDS AND I WILL REDUCE YOU TO RANDOM MOLECULES.
SHOW ME YOUR SKILL, KREED. THE WEAPONS CONSOLE LIES BENEATH THAT PANEL. USE WHAT IS THERE TO DISABLE, BUT CAUSE NO DEATHS IF YOU CAN HELP IT.
YES! EXQUISITE!
PHOTONS TORP.
LASER FIRE
YOUR SACRED MISSION PRECLUDES DEATH FOR THOSE WHO DON'T DESERVE IT! I WILL SHOW YOU HOW THE QUATROS FIGHT!
NEXUS--YOU PROMISED US A KILLING SPREE!
I MADE NO PROMISES, MR. TWILLY. IF YOU LIKE DEATH SO MUCH YOU CAN ALWAYS RETURN TO CHERNENKO.
I'LL USE THE SPECIFIC FOCUS LASERS TO SEAL THEIR WEAPONS PORTS. HAH! WATCH ME NOW!

I HAVE CROSSED THE GALAXY TO LEARN YOUR WAYS.
ZZZT
HAVE YOU, MR. TWILLY?
WHAT IS THE SOURCE OF YOUR POWER?
ZZT
WHAT DO YOU THINK? WHAT ARE YOUR THEORIES?
ZZZT
I KNOW NOT WHAT TO THINK. THIRTY-SIX HOURS WE HAVE SHARED THESE CRAMPED QUARTERS, AND I HAVE SEEN NO POWER. ONLY YOUR FLAWLESS DISPLAY OF ARROGANCE.
INCOMING! FOUR STAGGERED HOMERS! GRAB HOLD!
8

KREED! I THOUGHT YOU WERE INFALLIBLE.
FORGIVE ME, GREAT ONE! THESE CONTROLS ARE NEW TO ME AND OUT OF TUNE!
BUT THE SHIP IS UNTOUCHED! I HARDLY FELT THE SHOCK! WHAT MANNER OF FORCE FIELD DO YOU EMPLOY?
TAKE A GUESS.
DO YOU ALWAYS ANSWER A QUESTION WITH A QUESTION?
I AM NOT HERE TO ANSWER YOUR QUESTIONS. I LET YOU COME BECAUSE YOU ARE KREED'S FRIEND.
WILL YOU LET KREED DO ALL THE WORK?
IT IS HIS PLEASURE.
THREE HEAVY CRUISERS IN HOT PURSUIT... STAND BY FOR HEAVY WEATHER!
RADIATION AND RESIDUE FROM THAT LEAD CRUISER WILL CONFUSE OUR PURSUERS LONG ENOUGH FOR US TO ELUDE THEM.
BUT KREED VIOLATES YOUR DICTUM! THERE ARE BOUND TO BE CASUALTIES! LOOK--YOU CAN SEE THEM!
IT WAS NOT A DICTUM, MR. TWILLY. IT WAS A REQUEST.

NEXUS HAS PENETRATED THE SPHERE OF SATURN! NINETEEN SHIPS DISABLED, ONE HEAVY CRUISER DESTROYED.
MR. PRESIDENT, MIGHT IT NOT BE WISER TO RELOCATE TO SOME REMOTE AREA... WITH LESS CHANCE OF CIVILIAN CASUALTIES?
WHAT?! DESERT THE CAPITAL IN ITS HOUR OF NEED?! I SHOULD SAY NOT!!
BUT MR. PRESIDENT! HE'S AFTER YOU!
THAT IS A GROUNDLESS ASSERTION! DO YOU ACCUSE ME OF MURDER?!
THE OLD FOOL'S STANDING PAT. WHAT NEXT?
WE HAVE NO CHOICE. ON MY SIGNAL...
NOW!
ZAT ZAT
YAHH!!
ZZZZZATT!
WHAT?
ZOW
HE'S GOT HIS FORCE FIELD UP! WHAT NOW?
GUARDS! GUARDS!
KEEP FIRING! WE WON'T GET A SECOND CHANCE!
ZAK
YARRGH!
AHH!
ZAK
THANK GOD!
SECURITY
SECURITY
10

JUST OUTSIDE THE SPHERE OF MARS.
OBSERVE, GREAT ONE. THE LARGEST DEFENSE EVER MOUNTED WITHIN THE WEB--ALL FOR ONE MAN! OUR MISSION RESONATES!
IF THESE FOOLS INSIST ON THROWING THEMSELVES AGAINST US THERE WILL BE MORE NEEDLESS SLAUGHTER.
WHY DO YOU AVOID THEM? LET THEM FEAR GREAT NEXUS' MIGHT!
NO, TWILLY. DEATH BY HIS HAND IS TOO PRECIOUS A GIFT TO THROW AWAY ON THOSE UNDESERVING.
LET THE HEAVENS BESTOW A GLOWING ORNAMENT, THAT WE MAY PROCEED TO EARTH BY INDIRECTION!
CRACK!
CRACK!
SOMEWHERE BETWEEN MARS AND JUPITER, A PINPRICK OF LIGHT APPEARS...
EXPLODING INTO A GLOWING NIMBUS OF ICE AND ROCK-- A COMET!

INSTANTLY IT SPEEDS TOWARD EARTH, WITHOUT BENEFIT OF ACCELERATION, AS IF EXEMPT FROM THE LAWS OF PHYSICS.
A FREAK OCCURENCE-- IT MUST HAVE BEEN TRAPPED BY A SINGULARITY AND POPPED OUT HERE...
IT'S 50 KILOMETERS WIDE... I DON'T BELIEVE IN COINCIDENCE, MAJOR ZORN. DESTROY IT!
NEXUS IS INSIDE THAT COMET!
WHILE THE MARTIAN FLEET ARRAYS ITSELF AGAINST THE COMET, A NIXXON TANKER PROCEEDS ON COURSE FROM THE ASTEROIDS TOWARD EARTH'S MOON.
THERE THEY GO...
HOLOGRAM COMBINED WITH FORCE FIELD CREATE AN IDENTIFIABLE SHAPE --A SLOW MOVING TANKER.
QUITE A BIT OF TRAFFIC TODAY.
YOU SURPRISE ME. HAVE YOU USED THIS SUBTERFUGE BEFORE?
NO. THIS IS THE TYPE OF GAG YOU CAN USE ONLY ONCE. AFTER THAT THEY'LL FIGURE IT OUT.
BUT WHY BOTHER? WHY NOT JUST PUNCH STRAIGHT THROUGH AS YOU DID ON ROSARIO, WHEN YOU KILLED ZIEFFER?
12

EACH JOURNEY IS A WORK OF ART, MR. TWILLY. EACH KILLING TO BE CARVED ANEW.
THERE! YOU SEE? YOU SEE?!
BUT IF SOMETHING FORCES YOU OUT...
WHAT FORCE?
I DO THIS OF MY OWN FREE WILL!
ENOUGH! IF I HAD KNOWN YOU WERE GOING TO HASSLE GREAT NEXUS, I WOULDN'T HAVE INVITED YOU! THIS IS NOT A CELEBRITY LUNCH!
NO--WAIT. YOU MUST EXCUSE ME, MR. TWILLY.
I HAVEN'T BEEN MYSELF LATELY. I HAVE BEEN A BAD HOST.
HOST?
THIS IS THE MOST SOLEMN MISSION! THIS IS NO AMUSEMENT RIDE!
BUT SOMETIMES I FORGET TO OBSERVE THE AMENITIES. ASK WHAT YOU WILL, MR. TWILLY. I WILL DO MY BEST TO ANSWER.
IS IT TRUE THE KILLERS APPEAR TO YOU IN DREAMS?

YES... THEY COME LEERING AT ME OUT OF THE DARKNESS... AS THEY APPEARED TO THEIR VICTIMS ...I SEE IT ALL AND FEEL IT ALL...
SUPPOSE HE HAS CAUSED A THOUSAND DEATHS...I HAVE LIVED THEM, EVERY ONE. CAN YOU IMAGINE WHAT IT'S LIKE?

TO COMPRESS ALL THAT SUFFERING--SPREAD ACROSS A DECADE OR MORE--INTO A SINGLE DREAM?
I HAVE AGED A THOUSAND YEARS IN A NIGHT.
THERE CAN BE NO DOUBT, GENERAL KROGH DESERVED TO DIE.
ME TOO, PROBABLY.

DOCKING THE STILL-DISGUISED SHIP ON THE MOON, NEXUS AND COMPANY BOARD THE EARTH SHUTTLE.
SHUTTLE
DESTINATION
NEW YORK
PEKING
PHOBOS
AST 6
VENUS

I FAIL TO SEE WHY YOU DO NOT SIMPLY WALK IN AND DO THE JOB DETROIT STYLE.
RELAX, KREED. THINK OF THIS AS A VACATION.
LOOK AT MR. TWILLY --FASCINATED BY EVERYTHING HE SEES...
I HAVE NEVER BEEN TO EARTH BEFORE.
TOMATO JUICE

INSIDE THE CAPITAL BUILDING.
GREETINGS. WHEN DOES THE NEXT TOUR BEGIN?
SIR, YOU'RE JUST IN TIME.
Welcome to
CAPITAL
Tours
INC

HERE IS OUR TRAPEZOIDAL OFFICE, WHERE THE PRESIDENT RECEIVES DIPLOMATS FROM TAU CETI...
NEXT DOOR, THE HEXAGONAL OFFICE...
14

HERE, THE PRESIDENT RECEIVES QUATROS AND RACKNIDS... THEY GET ***DIZZY*** IN SQUARE ROOMS...
OPEN IT.
BUT IT'S JUST A SERVICE CORRIDOR.

YOU SEE? A CLEANING CLOSET.
A SQUARE CLEANING CLOSET.
IF YOU WISH TO LEAVE ME, DO IT NOW. FROM HERE ON THERE IS NO TURNING BACK.
YOU WILL BE BRANDED THROUGHOUT THE WEB.
WE ARE WITH YOU.
SO BE IT.

OH MY GOD--
HE'S IN THE
BUILDING!
WHAT?! WHAT DID SHE SAY?!
RELAX, MR. PRESIDENT.
I TOLD YOU TO KEEP YOUR VOICE DOWN!

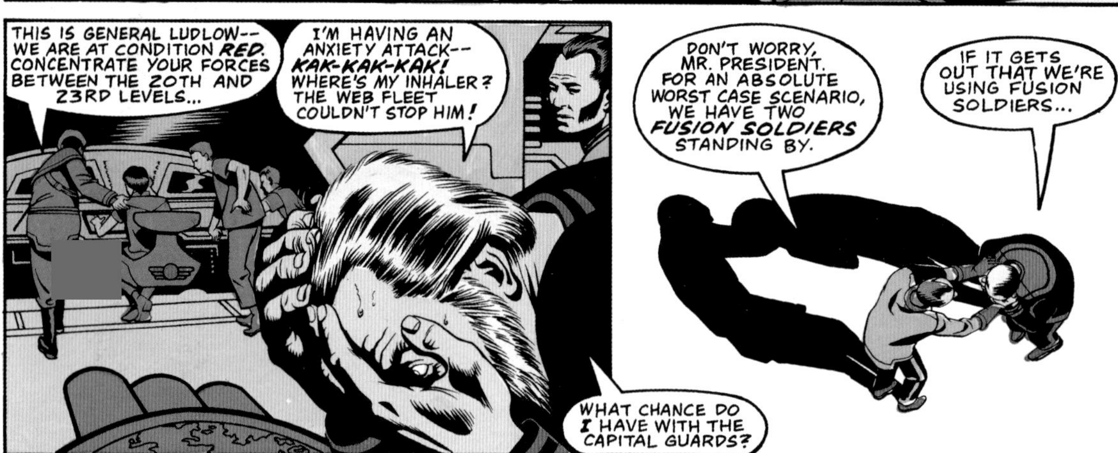
THIS IS GENERAL LUDLOW--
WE ARE AT CONDITION RED.
CONCENTRATE YOUR FORCES
BETWEEN THE 20TH AND
23RD LEVELS...
I'M HAVING AN ANXIETY ATTACK-- KAK-KAK-KAK! WHERE'S MY INHALER? THE WEB FLEET COULDN'T STOP HIM!
WHAT CHANCE DO I HAVE WITH THE CAPITAL GUARDS?
DON'T WORRY, MR. PRESIDENT. FOR AN ABSOLUTE WORST CASE SCENARIO, WE HAVE TWO FUSION SOLDIERS STANDING BY.
IF IT GETS OUT THAT WE'RE USING FUSION SOLDIERS...

SCANNER
VROOM!
RED ALERT
IT WON'T. YOU'LL SEE. HERE'S YOUR PERSONAL BODYGUARD.
THE WEB CAN'T HOLD WITHOUT ME! I PUT IT TOGETHER! MY GENIUS! MY PLANNING!

YOU UNDERSTAND THE SITUATION, MAJOR? LOSE THAT BEAMER. USE YOUR HANDS. BURN HIM OUT IF YOU HAVE TO, BUT STOP HIM.
YES SIR.
MY ENEMIES ARE GANGING UP ON ME!

HOW MANY HEADS?
20,000. ALL VOLUNTEERS. THEY'RE PLUGGED INTO THE SUN. IF THIS GOES ON TOO LONG, THERE COULD BE SOME REAL UGLY SIDE-EFFECTS.
16

DON'T WORRY, MAJOR. WE'LL BACK OFF RATHER THAN PUT THE SOLAR SYSTEM IN PERIL.
HISTORY WILL ABSOLVE ME! YOU'LL SEE! HISTORY WILL BE MY JUDGE!
ALVIN! LOOK HOW CLOSE HE IS!
HE'S HERE!
GO! FIRE! KILL HIM!
DEFENSE SECTOR
WHERE ARE OUR BACK-UPS?
17

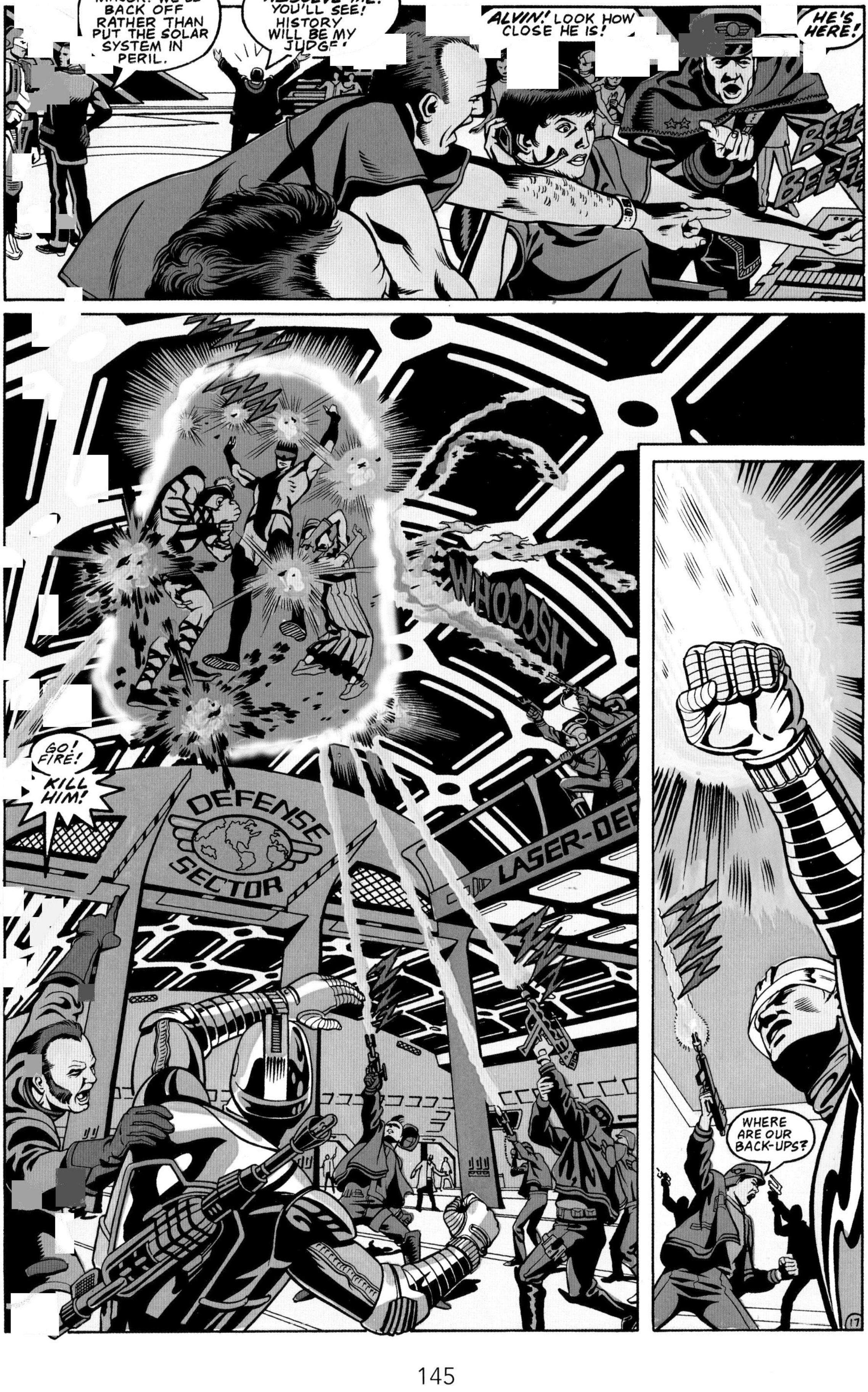

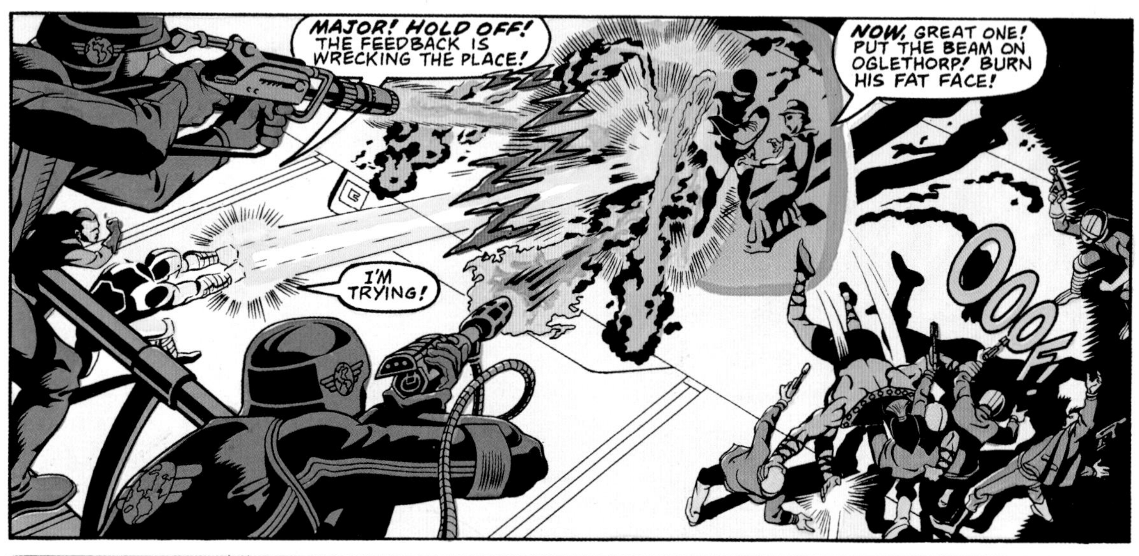
MAJOR! HOLD OFF! THE FEEDBACK IS WRECKING THE PLACE!
NOW, GREAT ONE! PUT THE BEAM ON OGLETHORP! BURN HIS FAT FACE!
I'M TRYING!
OOOF!

NOW, DID YOU SAY, MR. TWILLY?
YES! YES!
AND THEN YOU DIE! MY FINGER IS ON THE BUTTON-- I HAVE BUT TO STEP INTO THE ENERGY FLOW AND REVERSE IT!

THEN WALK WITH ME... SEE HOW IT'S DONE.
BACK OFF, MAJOR!
I CAN'T!

BAWOOM
STOP! WHAT ARE YOU DOING?
I'M SHOWING YOU HOW IT'S DONE.
18

AFTER ALL, I'M A REALIST...
YOU CANNOT HARM ME, FOR I AM INDISPENSABLE TO THE FUTURE OF THE WEB.
I KNOW THAT WE MUST DEAL CONSTANTLY FROM A POSITION OF STRENGTH...
IT IS EVEN A GOOD THING TO APPEAR SOMEWHAT CRAZED TO OUR ENEMIES...
BLAM
YOU KNOW!
IT WAS PAINFULLY OBVIOUS THAT YOU WERE WAITING FOR A CHANCE TO HARNESS MY POWER AGAINST ME.
BUT ONE DOES NOT LOOK TO THE SOVS FOR SUBTLETY.
KREED, WILL YOU REMOVE THIS GARBAGE?
WITH PLEASURE.
HERE, TWILLY. TAKE BACK YOUR GIFT.
PLEASE CONVEY MY CONGRATULATIONS TO THE VICE PRESIDENT.

HOW DID YOU KNOW TWILLY WAS A SOV ASSASSIN?
I ASKED ONE OF THE GIZ-TYPE HEADS TO RUN A MIND SCAN ON HIM. I DO NOT TRAVEL WITH SUSPICIOUS STRANGERS.
HAVE YOU EVER DONE THIS TO ME?
NO.
I TRUST YOU. I DON'T KNOW WHY. BUT I DO.
THERE IS YLUM.
SOON...
YOU HAVE HOUSE GUESTS.
WHO?
SHE ASKED NOT TO BE IDENTIFIED. I MEAN HE! HE ASKED NOT TO BE IDENTIFIED!
SUNDRA?
I DON'T BELIEVE IT!
YLUM RECEPTION
BELIEVE IT.
NEXT MONTH
JUDAH THE HAMMER
&

CYGNUS 7-- A WAY STATION ON THE ROAD TO STARDOM.
SORRY, MR. CLONEZONE, SIR, THE EPIPHANY SHUTTLE HAS BEEN SUCKED UNDER. IT COULD BE 19 HOURS BEFORE WE HAVE A REPLACEMENT.
FINE, BEAUTIFUL, SWELL, TERRIFIC! STUCK IN THIS SWELTERING HELL HOLE! I CAN REVIEW MY LIFE!
SO POINT ME TO THE CASINO, IT SHOULDN'T BE A TOTAL LOSS.
SORRY, MR. CLONEZONE, SIR, NO CASINO.
YO YO MA! NO CASINO? WHAT ABOUT A LOUNGE?
VANCE, J.H.
NO LOUNGE.
HOW ABOUT A LOUNGER?
FOR YOUR CONVENIENCE, ALL OUR SLEEPING ACCOMODATIONS ARE TEMPORARILY OUT OF ORDER. UNLESS YOU'RE AMPHIBIOUS.
BAR?
NO BAR.
WAIT! A CABANA, AT LEAST...
YES, WE HAVE NO CABANAS.
GLEEP! EVENTS HAVE REACHED A NADIR... I COULD JUST ABOUT RALPH...
THINGS CAN'T GET ANY WORSE.
WELL WELL WELL ...

TALES from the CLONEZONE
TM
AN ENCOUNTER
MIKE BARON · STORY
MARK A. NELSON · ART
STEVE HAYNIE · LETTERS
LES DORSCHEID · COLORS
RICK OLIVER · EDITS
IF IT ISN'T THE MUCH DECLAIMING CLONEZONE, PURVEYOR OF BRUISED HUMOR...
JOKIN' JOHNNY JERKOWITZ! YOU WORKING THIS TOILET?
NAHH... I'M WAITING FOR THE SCHAPP SHUTTLE...
SO, ZONE... YOU STILL WORKIN' THE CATSKILL ASTEROIDS?
WHO, ME? YOU MUST BE OUT OF TOUCH. I JUST CUT A SIX PIC DEAL WITH 26TH CENTURY...
DOIN' WHAT? BEST BOY? CHIEF GAFFER? WARDROBE GOFER?
MOST HUMOROUS, JOHNNY. MY BOWELS ARE IN AN UPROAR.
PROTEIN? LIQUID? ZAG? RUN? MEKLE? KLACKTOVEED-ESTEEN?
SO I'M TALKIN' TO THIS GOMER FROM VERDANT--THAT'S A NEW COLONY ON TITAN.
I KNOW WHERE VERDANT IS. THOSE PEOPLE ARE SO DUMB THEY THINK GROUND ZERO IS A GRADE OF CHOPPED BEEF.
2

YOU AIN'T **KIDDIN'!** SO I'M TALKIN' TO THIS GOMER AND HE'S TRYING TO EXPLAIN THE TWO MOST SOLEMN TENETS OF THEIR RELIGION...

"YOUR CHECK IS IN YOUR MOUTH, AND I WON'T COME IN THE MAIL."

PNUME EATING HABITS

I KNOW WHAT YOU MEAN. RAN INTO A BUNCH OF FRISBYTERIANS LAST WEEK. THEY WORSHIP THOSE LITTLE PLASTIC PIE TINS?
DIRDIR DANCING LESSONS: A
fantastic!! C.A. SMITH

RIGHT. THEY THINK THAT WHEN YOU DIE, YOUR SOUL GOES UP ON THE ROOF AND YOU CAN'T GET IT DOWN.

WHAT CAN YOU EXPECT FROM A PEOPLE WHOSE NATIONAL SYMBOL IS THE PET ROCK?
I THOUGHT THAT WAS THEIR NATIONAL **FLOWER**.
IT **IS** THE NATIONAL FLOWER. IT'S ALSO THE OFFICIAL FOOD AND CURRENTLY SERVING A TERM AS PRESIDENT.
SNAP CRACKLE POP

WHO'S VICE-PRESIDENT? **TWO** PET ROCKS?
HEY, YOU'RE GETTING SILLY.
JUST **NOW** I'M GETTING SILLY?
3

LISTEN, I'LL BUY YOU A BEVERAGE.
THAT'S SWELL OF YOU, JOKIN' JOHN--I TAKE IT BACK WHAT I SAID ABOUT YOU BEING SO CHEAP YOU ATE WEEK-OLD WONDERBREAD AND DEAD PIGEON SANDWICHES. I KNEW IT WAS A LIE BECAUSE YOU'RE ALLERGIC TO WONDERBREAD.
ZONE, YOU WOUND ME. THE TRUTH IS I GOT A STOMACH CONDITION-- LAST NIGHT I DREAMED I ATE A GIANT MARSHMALLOW AND WHEN I WOKE UP MY PILLOW WAS GONE.
HEY, MY HOTEL ROOM ON ARCTURUS WAS SO SMALL, YOU HAD TO EAT THE PILLOW TO MAKE ROOM TO SLEEP!
LAST PLACE I WAS IN, I SEE THIS FLY DOING A BREASTSTROKE THROUGH MY MINESTRONE-- WAITER TRIED TO TELL ME IT WAS A TIME-SHARE BOWL.
I ALWAYS BRING MY OWN FLY--I DON'T LIKE UNPLEASANT SURPRISES. YOU GET A SLOPPY FLY, IT CAN RUIN THE WHOLE MEAL.
ABSOLUTELY. YOU CAN LEAD A WHORE TO CULTURE BUT YOU CAN'T MAKE HER THINK.
EXACTLY.
OR, TO PUT IT ANOTHER WAY, LIFE IS LIKE A COLOSTOMY BAG --WHAT YOU GET OUT OF IT DEPENDS ON WHAT YOU PUT INTO IT.
I THOUGHT LIFE WAS A HOLE INTO WHICH YOU POURED MONEY.
NO, THAT'S A BOAT.
SPEAKIN' OF WHICH, I HEAR YOU MADE QUITE A SPLASH AT THE LAFF LOUNGE...
I SANK WITHOUT A RIPPLE! THE LAFF LOUNGE IS ABOUT AS CONDUCIVE TO LAUGHTER AS A TOTAL VACUUM IS TO A SALMON SOUFFLE!
TOUGH?! LAST CYCLE I WORKED A SEPTIC TANK CALLED GAZORNINBLATT'S. THAT PLACE WAS SO TOUGH, YOU GOT AIDS JUST LOOKING AT THE DOORKNOBS! THE MANAGER ISSUED ME A BAZOOKA AND A BLASTER AND TOLD ME I WAS ON MY OWN!
THE ONLY WAY TO GET A LAUGH WAS TO DRILL SOMEBODY!
THAT ALWAYS GETS A LAUGH.
MR. CLONEZONE, MR. JERKOWITZ...
4

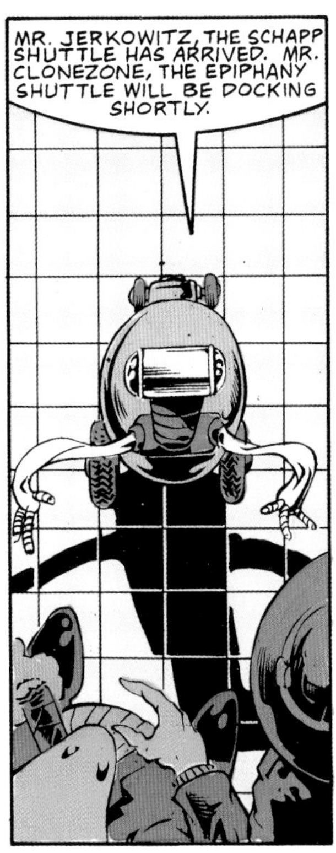
MR. JERKOWITZ, THE SCHAPP SHUTTLE HAS ARRIVED. MR. CLONEZONE, THE EPIPHANY SHUTTLE WILL BE DOCKING SHORTLY.

WELL, JOHNNY-- IT'S BEEN A PLEASURE AND AN HONOR. WE MUST TAKE DINNER TOGETHER SHORTLY ...BRING YOUR OWN FLY.
YASS... WHERE YOU HEADED FROM HERE, ZONE?

AH, THREE WEEKS AT THE COPA ON CYGNUS 1. I'M HEADLINING--THE TREPITDATIONS AND SIMPLAMENTE ARE OPENING.
YOU?
AH, I'M OPENING IN A REVIVAL OF "DEATH OF AN ENTIRE SOLAR SYSTEM" AT THE ROXY ON TITAN. WE'RE SOLD OUT FOR 19 CYCLES.
WELL, DROP DEAD, PAL!

ADIEU, DEAR FRIEND! I MUST CATCH YOUR ACT NEXT TIME!
LIKEWISE ...

THE EPIPHANY SHUTTLE.
HA! IF THAT CANNED SPAM IS STARRING IN "DEATH OF AN ENTIRE SOLAR SYSTEM," I'M A PLATE OF SPAGHETTI-O'S!

THE SCHAPP SHUTTLE.
MANNY, IF THAT CROCK OF CROCK IS HEADLINING AT THE COPA ON CYGNUS, I'M EMPEROR OF SIAM.
FORGET THE LIZARD, JJJ, AND CLUE INTO THIS... THIS DUMP YOU'RE PLAYING? THEY GOT A NINE LAUGH PER HOUR MINIMUM. AFTER THAT, DOWN COMES THE FORCE FIELD AND THEY CAN HIT YA!
5

HI! HOW YOU ALL DOIN' TONIGHT? ANYONE FROM McKEESPORT OUT THERE?

GRRR--!!

GRRRR..!

HISSSSSSss...

GULP I HEARD YOU GUYS ARE SO CHEAP, YOU EAT WEEK-OLD WONDERBREAD AND DEAD PIGEON SANDWICHES...

6

HERE HE IS, FOLKS, THAT FRANKLY HILARIOUS LIZARD, CLONEZONE!

THANKS, STU-- GREETINGS, GENTLE SENTIENTS... AND WELCOME TO GAZORNINBLATT'S, HOME OF THE DO-IT-YOURSELF APPENDECTOMY...

GRRR--!

GRRR--!

HISSSSSSS...

PLPLPLPL!

I'M SORRY... I FORGOT THE TWO MOST SOLEMN PROMISES ON EPIPHANY... "YOUR CHECK IS IN YOUR MOUTH..."

GRRR--!

...THE NATIONAL, FLOWER, OFFICIAL FOOD, AND CURRENTLY SERVING A TERM AS VICE-PRESIDENT!

... AND WHEN I WOKE UP, MY PILLOW WAS GONE!

MR. CLONEZONE, SIR, I'M FROM THE LOCAL PAPER... COULD I BUY YOU A DRINK?

12M
8M
FLIPPER 5000
SEA & SKI
BREW

TWICE EACH EARTH YEAR, JUDAH MACCABEE MUST SEPARATE HIMSELF FROM THE FUSION POWER GENERATED BY HIS PARTNERS, THE TELEKINETIC HEADS, LEST THE CONCENTRATED ENERGY CAUSE HIS NERVOUS SYSTEM TO BURN OUT.
NEXUS®
BATEMAN, THE SHIP IS IN YOUR HANDS. SEE YOU IN 1.5 CYCLES.
HAVE A GOOD TIME, HAMMER.
Yo! Jimbo!
BORN TO VACATION-- WE WERE! BORN TO VACATION!
WRITER: MIKE BARON
GUEST ARTIST: ERIC SHANOWER
COLORIST: LES DORSCHEID
LETTERER: STEVE HAYNIE
EDITOR: RICK OLIVER
"It's bad enough when you bow to fads like the ninja craze, but this is simply too much." –William Smith, in a letter to Inside Kung Fu
AH, FIONA! SWEETEST VACATION SPOT IN THE ASTEROID BELT! AN UNSPOILED PARADISE OF FUN, SUN, SAND, SURF, AND TURF! HOW I LOOK FORWARD TO RELAXATION!

SAFELY ENCLOSED IN A PLASTISPHERE, JUDAH RELAXES WHILE THE SPHERE'S GUIDANCE SYSTEM DRAWS HIM TOWARD THE PLUSH RESORT.

ROUGHING IT
MARK TWAIN

AH! JUST **LOOK** AT THAT SPARKLING WATER! I CAN PRACTICALLY TASTE THOSE SUCCULENT SNAILS!

FLINN THE INNKEEPER! HOW THE HECK ARE YOU?

WELCOME, HAMMER! WELCOME TO FLINN'S INN FIONA! I'M SUFFERING FROM HYPERTENSION, NAUSEA, AND POSSIBLY AN ULCER.

BUT FLINN--WHAT COULD GO WRONG ON FIONA?

PLENTY. WE HAVE NO GOVERNMENT OR LAW. TECHNICALLY, WE'RE UNDER **WEB** PROTECTION. BUT THAT DIDN'T STOP THE **PESTO NUESTRO** FROM SETTING UP SHOP.

THE PESTO NUESTRO?

CRIME SYNDIC--GOT THEIR TAILS BOOTED OFF PHOBOS SO THEY SETTLED HERE.

NOT AT **THIS** HOTEL, ALVIN FORFEND!

NOT EXACTLY ...

2

THEY HAVE THEIR OWN PLACE ABOUT 30 KILOMETERS FROM HERE. UNFORTUNATELY, THEY'VE TAKEN A LIKING TO FLINN'S FINE CUISINE...
AND WHO CAN BLAME THEM?
SEEMS FIONA IS IDEALLY SITUATED FOR ARMS MERCHANTS SERVING THOSE FIGHTIN', FEUDIN', FEUDAL ASTEROIDS...

BUT THAT'S ONLY HALF OF IT! SOON AFTER THE PESTOS SETTLED IN, **ANOTHER** CRIME SYNDIC, THE **RORSCHACH BLOTS**, DECIDED TO SET UP SHOP.
THEY LIKE MY MENU, TOO... **AND** THE MUSIC, **AND** THE POOL...

UNFORTUNATELY, THE BLOTS AND THE PESTOS DO **NOT** LIKE EACH OTHER. AND **I'M** CAUGHT IN THE MIDDLE.
I SEE...

WELL WELL... BERYL, WILL YOU LOOK AT THIS?
FRESH BLOOD.

NO, I'M CERTAIN I HAVE A RESERVATION...
CRUNCH

IF YOU'LL BEAR WITH ME WHILE MR. FLINN CHECKS HIS RECORDS, I'LL SHOW YOU...
WHOOF
JUDAH! THEY'RE PACKING!

OH BOTHER! I LEFT ALL MY GUNS AT HOME!
ZAP
SMASH

THANKS FOR THE JUICE, FOOL!
YAHH!

AND NOW, MY FRIEND, IT'S TIME FOR YOU TO GO...
4

ADIOS!
VOOOOOOM!
WELL, FLINN, THOSE PESTOS SHOULD BOTHER YOU NO MORE.
THEY WON'T BOTHER ANYONE ANY MORE.

AH...THIS IS THE LIFE! GOOD FOOD, GOOD WINE, AND A GOOD BOOK...
YO! JIMBO!

VERILY, IF I MUST KILL SOMEBODY TO ENJOY A MODICUM OF PEACE, SO BE IT!
NO--JIMBO--YOU GOT IT ALL WRONG! I'M BARRY OF THE BLOTS! MY BOYS TOLD ME WHAT YOU DID TO THOSE PESTO JERKS...
HMMM...

MUNCH!
HEY--THOSE GUYS WERE PUNKS! A THUNE OF YOUR TALENTS --YOU SHOULD BE WORKING FOR ME! WHAT'S YOUR NAME, PAL?
JUDAH MACCABEE...
WELL MR. MACCABEE--HOW WOULD YOU LIKE TO JOIN THE BLOTS?
WHAT WOULD I DO?

A LITTLE A-DIS-A, A LITTLE A-DAT-A, WITH AN EMPHASIS ON DE LATTA!
5

WHAT DO YOU SAY, MR. MACCABEE? ¤1000 PER CYLE TO START. HERE'S ONE CYCLE IN ADVANCE --GO GET YOURSELF SOME DECENT DUDS AND DROP BY THE RORSCHACH SHACK TONIGHT--WE'RE HAVING A LITTLE PARTY.
HMMM ...
NARROW LAPELS, RIGHT?
HA HA! YOU GOT IT!

I DON'T GET IT, JUDAH. THOSE BLOTS ARE VILE! DRUGS, MURDER--NOTHING'S TOO DIRTY FOR THEM. WHY WOULD YOU TAKE A JOB WITH THEM?
UNLAX, FLINN! UNLA-A-AXX! NOT ONLY CAN I GET THIS VACATION TO PAY FOR ITSELF, I MIGHT EVEN HAVE A SOLUTION TO YOUR CURRENT DILEMMA.

WELL WATCH YOURSELF! I HEARD THE PESTOS HAVE GOT A HEAVY HITTER ON THE WAY--I THINK HE'S CALLED THE TASTER!
"THE TASTER?" WHERE DO YOU COME UP WITH THESE TIDBITS, FLINN?

IN THE RESTARAUNT --THEY DRINK, THEY TALK.
NATURALAMENTE.

6

GREETINGS-- JUDAH MACCABEE --I'VE BEEN INVITED.
CERTAINLY. GO RIGHT IN, MR. MACCABEE. BARRY'S WAITING FOR YOU. EVAN WILL SHOW YOU THE WAY.
VALET PARKING
THIS WAY, SIR. PLEASE TAKE THE ELEVATOR TO THE OBSERVATORY.
HMMM... PARTYERS FROM MARS...
WEEE-HA!

AH, MR. MACCABEE..! OR HAMMER, IF YOU PREFER. I AM HUMILIATED THAT MY SO-CALLED "INTELLIGENCE" DID NOT LEARN OF YOUR EXTENSIVE REPUTATION UNTIL MERE HOURS AGO.
WELL, HERE I AM BARRY. WHAT'S UP?

HEY--RIGHT TO THE POINT! I LIKE THAT! OKAY! WE'VE GOT A DELICATE SITUATION VIS A VIS OUR COMPETITORS, THE PESTO NUESTRO.
WE CAN'T BOTH USE FIONA AS A DRUGS AND WEAPONS RANCH! WE'VE GOT TO DRIVE THE PESTOS OUT!
7

HMM. AND WHEN WOULD MONSIEUR LIKE TO EXECUTE THIS POLICY?
RIGHT NOW! JUDAH, THIS IS NIGEL. NIGEL, JUDAH. NIGEL IS MY CHIEF LIETENANT.

KRINK! CHOMP CHEW
440 STAINLESS MARS

GULP! YO.
NIGEL HAS AN IRON DEFICIENCY. HE'S ALWAYS CHEWING ON A MARS BAR.
WANT A PIECE? GNASH--GRIND
NO THANKS --I'M ON A DIET.

PTUI!
OH, I'M SORRY... I SEEM TO HAVE HAD A CERAMIC BALL LODGED IN MY MOUTH.
WHAM!
DON'T KILL MY MEN!
UNLAX, BARRY, HE'LL RECOVER-- EVENTUALLY. I GIVE YOU MY PERSONAL GUARANTEE --WE WON'T NEED HIM.
BENEATH THE EERILY REFLECTED LIGHT OF THE STARS, THREE STEALTH CRUISERS GLIDE INCHES ABOVE THE DESERT FLOOR.
THERE!

THOSE PESTOS ARE REAL SCUM! JUST LOOK AT THAT PILE OF CRAP! THEY DON'T EVEN KNOW HOW TO HAVE A GOOD TIME!
UNCULTURED LOUTS! WE BLOTS APPRECIATE FINE WINE, GREAT LITERATURE--
CLASSICS, LIKE HOLLYWOOD WIVES AND THE BOOK OF RANDOM NUMBERS!

BARRY--HOW DO WE GET PAST THE MASS-TRIGGERED FORCE FIELDS?
THAT'S WHERE OUR NEW ASSOCIATE COMES IN. HAMMER?

SSSSK
HOPE YOUR BATTERIES ARE FULLY CHARGED.

SNAP
CRACKLE
POP

HIT 'EM!
10

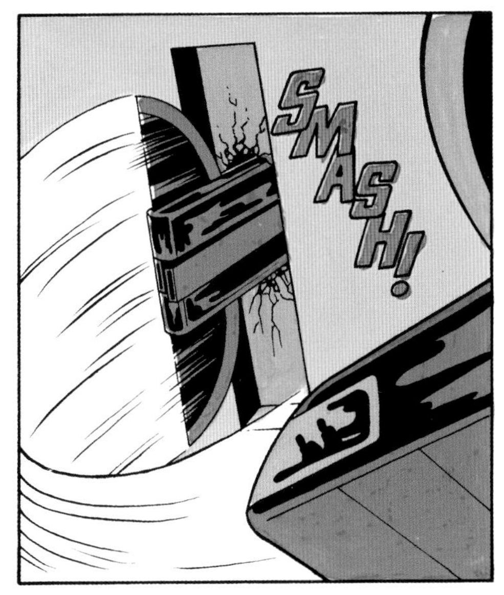
SMASH!

YO-YO MA!

HAMMER! GET AFTER LORD HARRY! KILL HIM AND WE CAN GET BACK TO THE PARTY!
NO SWEAT.

CHARGE!
MOP THE BLOTS!
BLOT 'EM OUT!
OH, HELL! THERE ARE MORE DAMN PESTOS THAN I THOUGHT!

NIGEL! PHONE BACK TO THE MANOR--GET REINFORCEMENTS! THEY'RE COMING OUT OF THE WOODWORK!
11

BARRY--LET'S GET THE HELL OUT OF HERE!
YO! FOLLOW THE HAMMER! HE'LL HAVE THE ROUTE CLEANED OUT.
ZAP!
THEN AGAIN... MAYBE NOT...
HEY PESTO! YOU JUST BOUGHT THE WHOLE BOX OF ROCKS!
FAP
WHAP
ZOOM
THUNK
12

UH, HI! WANT A JOB? DOUBLE WHAT THE PESTOS PAY!
I MEANT WHAT I SAID AND I SAID WHAT I MEANT-- AN ELEPHANT'S FAITHFUL, ONE HUNDRED PER...
PLAGIARIST!
AN INSULT FROM A FELLOW FIGHTER! I WAS JUST ABOUT TO NAME THE WRITER!
MY OLD FRIEND THE ANVIL-- I MIGHT HAVE KNOWN! "TASTER" IS A DISTORTION OF "POETASTER" AN INFERIOR POET!
GET HIM!

SNEER, FOOL! YOU ARE FEARFUL. THE BEAUTY OF THE SPOKEN WORD ESCAPES YOUR TINY BRAIN.
JACQUES--THAT'S NOT BAD! DID YOU WRITE THAT?
GET REAL. IT SUCKS!

THAT'S MINE--SO IS THIS: I ADVISE THE WISE MAN-- WISE MAN, LISTEN, THIS I SAY-- KEEP YOUR EYES ON THE BLUE HORIZON-- AND GLIDE YOU LIGHTLY THROUGH THE DAY!
WHY, JACQUES! THAT'S TRULY FINE!
ZAM
ARE YOU KIDDING?! THAT LINE WOULD GAG A DOG OFF A GUT WAGON!

BARRY FANCIES HE'S A CRITIC INSTEAD OF JUST ANOTHER SHALLOW THUG.
YES, I DEFINITELY DISCERN A NEW MATURITY IN YOUR WORDS AND YOUR DELIVERY!
WHACK

WELL-- YOU'RE A THUNE OF TASTE!
HOW DID YOU END UP WORKING FOR THESE PESTO CRACKERS?
14

HAMMER, YOU'RE A RIOT I CAME HERE FOR SOME PEACE AND QUIET. THIS USED TO BE A REAL NICE DIVE-- BEFORE THE PESTOS AND THE BLOTS ARRIVED.
THAT'S FUNNY--I CAME HERE FOR THE SAME REASON.

SAVE YOUR BREATH! IT'S TO THE DEATH!
BUT OF COURSE, JACQUES! HAPPY TO OBLIGE! BUT--I'M CURIOUS ...WHAT IS YOUR JOB DESCRIPTION ...EXACTLY?

OH NO! YOU TRICKED ME ONCE BEFORE--ALTHOUGH OUR CAUSE WAS LOST, YOU MADE ME COUGH UP CLAUSIUS!
YOU'RE TOO GOOD FOR ME NOW UNGH! I CAN SEE THAT...
WHAP

JUST TELL ME --WHAT DID LORD HARRY ASK YOU TO DO? ARE YOU HIS BODY-GUARD?
NO... OW! I'M SUPPOSED TO KILL BARRY... BARRY OF THE BLOTS. THAT'S ALL.
CRUNCH
15

THIS BARRY RIGHT HERE?
THAT'S THE ONE.
AND THERE'S NOTHING IN YOUR JOB DESCRIPTION ABOUT PROTECTING LORD HARRY?
NOT A WORD.
HEY, HAMMER!

YOU KNOW, JACQUES, I SEE A BRILLIANT SOLUTION TO ALL OUR PROBLEMS...
WHAT'S THAT?
HEY--! GAK!

I'VE BEEN HIRED TO KILL LORD HARRY! I SIMPLY PROPOSE WE STOP BANGING HEADS AND GET ON WITH OUR RESPECTIVE ASSIGNMENTS!

HERE.
I SAY, HAMMER-- THIS IS DAMNED DECENT OF YOU!
ULP!
CRUNCH

I WISH I COULD RECIPROCATE ...
NEVER MIND. I THINK I SEE LORD HARRY NOW.

YOU'RE NOT GOING TO CHASE HIM?
WHAT FOR? WHO'S PAYING?

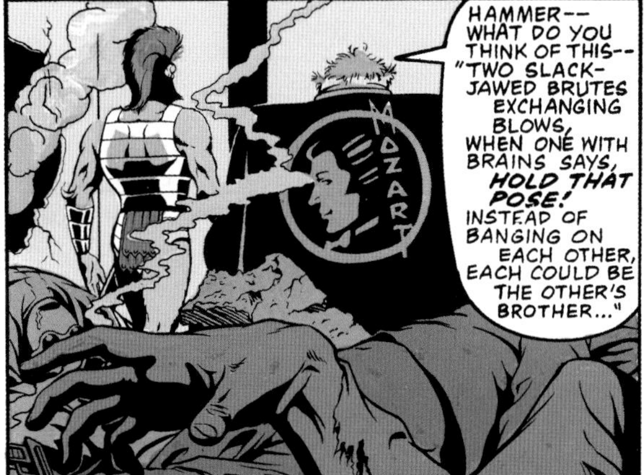
HAMMER-- WHAT DO YOU THINK OF THIS-- "TWO SLACK-JAWED BRUTES EXCHANGING BLOWS, WHEN ONE WITH BRAINS SAYS, HOLD THAT POSE! INSTEAD OF BANGING ON EACH OTHER, EACH COULD BE THE OTHER'S BROTHER..."
MOZART

YOU'RE GIFTED, JACQUES. I MEAN THAT SINCERELY. YOU SHOULD BE ON VID, ENTERTAINING BILLIONS... DO YOU HAVE PROFESSIONAL REPRESENTATION?
HAMMER, THIS COULD BE THE BEGINNING OF A BEAUTIFUL FRIENDSHIP...

LATER...
YOU SEE, FLINN, I TOLD YOU I'D CLEAR UP YOUR PROBLEM.
AND A REET SWEET JOB YOU'VE DONE OF IT. EVERYTHING IS ON THE HOUSE.
MR. FLINN, I'M HERE TO WIN. I'LL STICK WITH YOU THROUGH THICK AND THIN! JUST LET ME STAND UPON A STAGE, AND GNASH AND RAGE AND PICK AND GRIN.
17

I'LL ENTERTAIN YOUR HAPPY THRONGS-- I'LL SLING SOME RHYMES AND SING SOME SONGS--

YO! JIMBO!

WHOM MIGHT YOU BE ADDRESSING?
YOU, BIG GUY! YOU AND THE THUNE! YEAH! WE'RE THE BAKER'S DOZEN! WE HEARD HOW YOU GUYS WIPED OUT THE PESTOS AND THE BLOTS. YEAH! WE WANT TO SET UP SHOP HERE, AND HIRE YOU GUYS TO JOIN OUR GANG!
YOICKS. YOICKS, YOICKS, YOICKS.

WHOM MIGHT I BE ADDRESSING?
ME? I'M FAST EDDIE BAKER! YEAH!
AND ARE THE ENTIRE THIRTEEN OF YOU PRESENT?

YEAH, WELL, SORT OF! THE REST ARE OUT FRONT CHECKING IN. BUT THERE ARE ONLY ELEVEN OF US RIGHT NOW... THAT'S WHY WE'RE MAKING THIS FABULOUS OFFER!
COME, FLINN. LET US ASSIST THE NEW ARRIVALS.
18

JUDAH ASSISTS THE NEW ARRIVALS, NEATLY STACKING THE UNCONSCIOUS BODIES NEXT TO THEIR LUGGAGE.
WHOOSH

WHILE OUTSIDE BY THE POOL...
READ MY LIPS: FIONA IS OFF-LIMITS TO ANYONE DOING BUSINESS IN DRUGS, WEAPONS, OR SLAVES. I'M COUNTING ON YOU TO SPREAD THE WORD, EDDIE.
UH-HUNH! NO PROBLEM!

FLINN, I SEE A SIMPLE SOLUTION TO YOUR SITUATION.
I'M LISTENING.
FLINN'S INN FIONA PRESENTS, JACQUES BRAVO!!!!!!!!
SOME SAY FROST WAS A NASTY PIECE OF BUSINESS. SOME SAY HE WAS A SAINT. IT DOESN'T MATTER! WHAT MATTERS IS HOW HIS WORDS SPEAK TO US TODAY!
EXCEPT TO THOSE OF YOU WHO SPEAK NEITHER ENGLISH NOR INTERLAC, IN WHICH CASE THE NEXT QUARTER OF AN HOUR WILL SEEM LIKE GIBBERISH, FOR WHICH I APOLOGIZE.
19

NEXT MONTH: NEXUS RETURNS

TALES from the CLONEZONE™
CLONEZONES UNLIMITED
WORDS: MIKE BARON
PICTURES: MARK A. NELSON
LETTERS: STEVE HAYNIE
COLORS: LES DORSCHEID
DELETIONS: RICK OLIVER
KNOCK-KNOCK...

YOO-HOO--! HELLO--! ANYBODY HOME?
I JUST WANT TO USE THE BATHROOM... AND THE TRANSVID IF YOU HAVE ONE...

...AND MAYBE BORROW A HAMBURGER --I WILL GLADLY PAY YOU TUESDAY...
HMM... INTERESTING CONTRAPTION... SOME SORT OF MENTAL OR DENTAL REJUVENATOR ...

OH! I GET IT! IT'S A COMBINATION MENTAL/DENTAL REJUVENATOR AND MASSAGE UNIT! AID FOR THE BELEAGUERED LUMBAR REGION PLUS A SOOTHOMATIC SPINE STRAIGHTENER...

EEP!
OR--WHAT WE HAVE HERE IS A FLIGHT SIMULATOR DESIGNED TO TRAIN HYPER-SPACE PILOTS AND NEW YORK TAXI DRIVERS! VROOM! VROOM! VROOM WITH A VRIEW!

YOU... IDIOT! GET OUT OF THE STAGING AREA! WHAT ARE YOU DOING?! YOU MORON!

GAK! OKAY! OKAY! DON'T HAVE A HERNIA! I KNOCKED... I'M HARMLESS... AN ENTERTAINER... PERHAPS YOU'VE HEARD OF ME...

OUT!
ALL RIGHT ALREADY!

I'M ON MY WAY! I'LL GET A HAMBURGER ELSEWHERE!
oops...
CLICK!
DID YOU EVER HAVE THE FEELING THAT, THROUGH NO FAULT OF YOUR OWN, YOU HAVE BLUNDERED INTO AN ABSURD AND POSSIBLY HAZARDOUS SITUATION?
ONGGG-G-G-G-G!

TOO LATE NOW, YOU POOR BENIGHTED FOOL. IT'S ACTIVATED. YOU'LL JUST HAVE TO SIT THERE WHILE IT RUNS THROUGH A SIX CLONE CYCLE.
THAT'S THE MINIMUM. SIX CLONES.
CLANG
HONK
TWEET
BOINGGGGG
S-S-S-S-S-S-S-S-S-
BUZZ
BUZZ
2

OKAY--WHO STOLE MY SUITCASE?

MY SUITCASE! THE REST OF YOU GUYS ARE JUST A BUNCH OF D.T.'S!

SWELL! THERE'S ANOTHER ONE! DID JOKIN' JOHN PUT YOU GUYS UP TO THIS?

YOU KNOW, YOU DON'T LOOK SO GOOD...

DOC, I GOT A MAJOR HEADACHE!

3

OKAY, LISTEN UP, YOU CLOWNS! I'M THE ONE, THE ONLY, AND I'M GOING TO PROVE IT! YOU! WHERE WERE YOU BORN?
PUXATAWNEY, NEW JERSEY! WANNA MAKE SOMETHING OF IT?
WE GOT A SAYING IN PUXATAWNEY ...
"LIFE IS LIKE A COLOSTOMY BAG..."
"WHAT YOU GET OUT OF IT DEPENDS ON..."
SHADDUP! YOU'RE STEALING MY MATERIAL!
DOC, I'M BEGGIN'! HOW DO I GET RID OF THEM?
DON'T WORRY... WITHOUT THEIR BOOSTER SHOTS, THEY'LL FADE AWAY IN ABOUT A MONTH.
HEY! WHO'S THE EGG-HEADED GEEK?
MAYBE HE'S AN AGENT. CERTAINLY LOOKS LIKE AN AGENT.
A MONTH?!
HEY BUDDY --ARE YOU SUGARMAN THE AGENT? DON'T TALK TO JUST ONE OF US...
BACK OFF, FROG-BREATH. THIS IS A PRIVATE CONVERSATION.
YES, I'M SUGARMAN, AND I'M PREPARED TO MAKE YOU A VERY GENEROUS OFFER. IN FACT, I CAN MAKE OFFERS TO ALL OF YOU!
DOC! WHAT KIND OF GAME IS THIS?
OKAY YOU CLOWNS--! LISTEN UP! SUGARMAN HERE HAS BIG NEWS!
THAT'S RIGHT! CLONEZONE IS IN DEMAND! THEY WANT YOU ON BETELGEUSE, ARCTURUS, SCHAPP, TITAN, PHOBOS, DEIMOS, AND CLEVELAND!
ME!
NO, ME!
DIBS ON CLEVELAND!
I ALWAYS LIKED CLEVELAND.
4

WE'LL DRAW LOTS TO SEE WHO GOES WHERE.
SOUNDS FAIR TO ME.
ME TOO.
ME THREE.
ME FOUR.
ME TOO--AT LEAST I DON'T STEAL A LAME GAG LIKE THAT.
AND SO...
FAREWELL! BREAK LEGS! DROP DEAD! SINCERELY!
THANKS, SUGARMAN!
ONE HELL OF A SWEET GUY.
REALLY.
DOC--YOU'RE A GENIUS! LOVE YA! HOW CAN I EVER REPAY YOU?
I'LL TAKE 15% OF YOUR NEXT SIX GIGS.
DOC! THAT'S HIGHWAY ROBBERY!
SO!
NOW LOOK, YOU PUSHY BAG OF GATOR GUTS! I COULD SUE YOUR TAIL OFF FOR B&E, SCREWING UP MY EXPERIMENT, AND MALICIOUS MISCHIEF...
OKAY! OKAY! I WAS WRONG, I ADMIT IT! HOW DO YOU WANT TO WORK THIS?
I KNEW THAT WAS TOO EASY.
THE MOMENT MY BACK IS TURNED I FIND A FAKE ZONE, AND MY AGENT, WHO I THOUGHT WAS MY PAL, CONSPIRING AGAINST ME!
I WANT A PIECE OF THIS ACTION! MY MAMA DIDN'T RAISE NO DUMMIES!
YOU AIN'T GOT NO MAMA!
ALL RIGHT-- I WANT 15% OF BOTH YOUR NEXT SIX GIGS!

YOUR GENETIC CODE'S IN THE MACHINE NOW! EITHER YOU PAY OR I'LL CLONE THOUSANDS OF YOU! THE DEMAND WILL DROP TO ZERO! YOU'LL ALL BE OUT OF WORK!
SO!
DOC!
SUGARMAN, BABY!
THE MOMENT MY BACK IS TURNED, I FIND MY BEST FRIEND AND TWO OF MY CLONES CONSPIRING AGAINST ME!
GLEEP!
A FEW MINUTES LATER...
SO!
THAT'S RIGHT! 15% OF YOUR NEXT SIX GIGS-- ALL THREE OF YOU!
THE MOMENT MY BACK IS TURNED...
SHUT UP AND COME ON DOWN. THE DOC'S HAVING FLYERS PRINTED UP.
THAT'S THE DEAL! 15% OF YOUR NEXT SIX GIGS OR I FLOOD THE GALAXY WITH CHEAP CLONEZONES!
OKAY! HOLD YOUR WATER, DOC! WE HAVE TO TALK ABOUT THIS...
"CHEAP CLONEZONES?" THAT'S A REDUNDANCY.
HEY--YOU KNOW HOW TO KEEP A MORON IN SUSPENSE?
YEAH... I'LL TELL YOU LATER.
BUZZ-- MUMBLE-- GRUMBLE-- SNICKER
6

GET HIM! WE'LL TEACH THIS WISEGUY TO MESS WITH A COMEDY INSTITUTION!
NOT TO MENTION OUR ACTORS' EQUITY PENSION FUND!
WAIT! STOP YOU'LL REGRET THIS!

THAT'S RIGHT! STRAP HIM IN THAT CLONING CONTRAPTION!
NO! PLEASE! I BEG OF YOU!
I'M CRYING CROCODILE TEARS, SUGARMAN. CROCODILE TEARS.
MANNY CHEVRON'S GONNA HEAR ABOUT THIS, SUGAR. NONE OF YOU WILL EVER PLACE AN ACT IN VEGAS!

SORT OF REMINDS YOU OF ANGELS WITH DIRTY FACES, DOESN'T IT?
IT REMINDS ME I'M SUPPOSED TO PLAY CLEVELAND.
QUIT WHINING AND TAKE YOUR MEDICINE! HIT IT, BOYS!

ONE HOUR LATER.
I'M RUINED! THAT CLONING MACHINE WAS AN EXCLUSIVE!
I'M BLEEDING FOR YOU, SUGAR. NEVER CHISEL A CHISELLER.
AHA! HERE THEY ARE, MEN!
7

THERE YOU ARE, YOU WASHED-UP HAS-BEENS! WE **EACH** WANT 15% OF YOUR NEXT SIX GIGS OR WE'LL FLOOD THE GALAXY WITH **MILLIONS** OF CHEAP CLONEZONES!
BUT--BUT-- THAT'S 90% OF OUR EARNINGS!
TOUGH! I'M CRYING CROCODILE TEARS, CLONEZONE! CROCODILE TEARS!
INVADE A MAN'S HOME, WILL YOU?
I CAN'T STAND IT! I'M A SENSITIVE ARTISTE!

THERE HE GOES, MEN! AFTER HIM!
GRAB HIM! CLONE HIM AGAIN!
ALL I WANTED WAS TO USE THE VIDPHONE AND THE BATHROOM...

NO! NO! NO MORE ZONES!
ZONE! WAKE UP! YOU'RE HAVING A NIGHTMARE!

HUH?! OH! SUGAR BABY! WHEW! WHAT A **NIGHTMARE!** WHAT'S UP?
GOOD NEWS, ZONE. GOT A GIG FOR YOU IN CLEVELAND.

CLEVELAND? GREAT!
IN FACT, I HAVE GIGS FOR **ALL** OF YOU...
THE END...?
THE END...?
THE END...?

MY FAVORITE THUNES! WHY DIDN'T YOU TELL ME YOU WERE COMING?

IT'S A *SURPRISE*.

WE TOOK PAINS TO AVOID DETECTION.

DAVE

THE SITUATION ON YLUM IS CRITICAL. ARE YOU AWARE OF THE RECENT *CHANGE* THAT CAME OVER NEXUS?

YES. THE WHOLE GALAXY KNOWS. IT'S KIND OF HARD TO KEEP THE LID ON A *PRESIDENTIAL ASSASSINATION*.

ZZZZZ

WELD DROID

LEVEL

I WAS PLANNING TO CALL--I'M KIND OF ENTRENCHED HERE RIGHT NOW, BUT I'M HAPPY FOR HORATIO.

DON'T BE. HE IS *NOT* THE NEXUS OF OLD. THE THING THAT CONTROLS HIM HAS STRENGTHENED ITS GRIP.

DAVE

HE'S WORSE OFF THAN BEFORE. HE HAS *LOST* HIS CAPACITY TO FEEL *JOY*.

HE HAS BECOME THAT WHICH HE MOST *FEARED*...

A COLD-BLOODED KILLING MACHINE.

HE IS NOT HIMSELF--AND URSULA HAS JOINED HIM.
WHAT?!
INDEED, INDEED. WITH HER TWIN DAUGHTERS--BY NEXUS.
WHAT?!
WELD
DROID
GB-7

I KNOW NOT THE DETAILS. BUT THE MUST HAVE OCCURRED THREE EARTH YEARS AGO, WHEN HE RESCUED YOU FROM THE WEB.
MAYBE THERE WAS SOME KIND OF DEAL WITH URSULA--I...I... THIS IS TOO MUCH!

IF THAT'S WHAT HE WANTS, HE CAN HAVE IT.
IT'S NOT WHAT HE WANTS. WE TOLD YOU HE IS NOT HIMSELF.
AND ONLY YOU CAN SAVE HIM.
ME? HOW?
IT IS TIME TO CONFRONT THE ENTITY. BUT WHOEVER DOES SO SHOULD BE HUMAN. ALL HIS VICTIMS HAVE BEEN HUMAN.
WHY ME?
YOU LOVE HIM.
THUK
MAYBE I DID BEFORE...
JUDAH OR I WOULD DO IT, BUT WE ARE NOT HUMAN. THEREFORE, THE ENTITY WOULD DISCOUNT US.

SOON, HEADED ACROSS MARS.
WHY DO I NEED JUDAH TO GET IN THE DOOR?
JUDAH AND I WILL DO ANYTHING TO RESTORE NEXUS. JUDAH WILL GET YOU IN THE DOOR.
FOR KREED BARS THE GATE LIKE A COLOSSUS --AND NONE MAY ENTER.
ZIP SHIP
FUNSVILLE

NEXUS®
KREED AT THE GATE
"We killed the monster but the brain lives on."
– The Slickee Boys
GO AWAY!
MR. KREED, IF YOU DO NOT NOTIFY NEXUS OF OUR PRESENCE, I WILL HAVE TO ASK MY MEN TO REMOVE YOU.
DO IT!
REMOVE HIM!
writer: MIKE BARON
penciller: STEVE RUDE
inker: JOHN NYBERG
colorist: LES DORSCHEID
letterer: STEVE HAYNIE
editor: RICK OLIVER

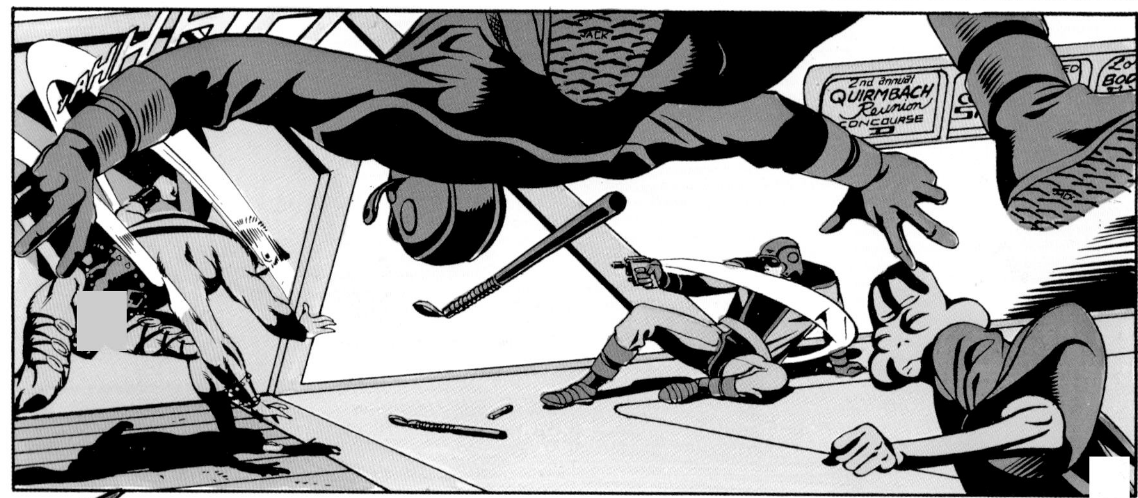
2nd annual
QUIRMBACH
Reunion
CONCOURSE
D

THUP
THUP
YAHH!
THUK

ALL LEVELS
GO AWAY! NONE MAY ENTER!
YOUR TIME IS NEARLY PAST, KREED.
THE BUREAUCRAT MOUTHS HOLLOW THREATS.

GO AWAY, YOU PRETTIFIED POLITICIAN. STAY TO THE UPPER LEVELS WHERE YOU ARE SAFE.
HOW ARE YOU, RACHMANINOFF?
I'LL MAKE IT.

OFFICE OF THE PRESIDENT.
RACHMANINOFF WAS LUCKY NOT TO LOSE AN ARM. WE CAN'T OVERLOOK THIS, MR. PRESIDENT. WE MUST ARREST KREED.
I DON'T THINK SO, SWERDLOW.
ARRESTING KREED WOULD MEAN A MAJOR MILITARY OPERATION. PEOPLE COULD GET KILLED.

FRANKLY, I CAN'T IMAGINE WHY YOU TRIED TO FORCE YOUR WAY IN THERE.
BUT, MR. PRESIDENT ...
THE LAW REQUIRES EVERY CITIZEN TO FILE A CENSUS SURVEY. NEXUS HASN'T COMPLIED WITH ANY OF THE NEW RULES! HE HAS IGNORED EVERY ENTREATY!
SWERDLOW, SWERDLOW... STOP TRYING TO ENFORCE THE LAW ON NEXUS. WE HAVE MORE PRESSING MATTERS.
THERE ARE 15,000 PEOPLE IN ORBIT AROUND YLUM WAITING TO APPLY FOR CITIZENSHIP. THEY'RE RUNNING OUT OF FOOD AND EVERYTHING ELSE...
UNSCRUPULOUS VENDORS ARE TAKING ADVANTAGE OF THEM.
YOU MEAN VOOPER?
5

VOOPER'S THE LEAST OF 'EM. THERE ARE SOME REGULAR PIRATES UP THERE. I WANT YOU TO SET UP AN EMERGENCY RELIEF SYSTEM... FIGURE OUT WHAT WE CAN SPARE AND GET TO IT.
RIGHT AWAY, MR. PRESIDENT.
ZIKK
WOULD YOU ASK CLAUDE TO COME IN?
MR. PRESIDENT.
MR. VICE PRESIDENT. HOW GOES THE EXPANSION?
WE'LL HAVE 500 CUBIC KILOMETERS OPEN THIS AFTERNOON.
ASTOUNDING WORK, CLAUDE! 500! HOW DID YOU DO IT?
I NEGOTIATED A DEAL--THE HEADS BROUGHT OVER A TERRAFORMING TEAM.
COME ON, MR. PRESIDENT. I'LL SHOW YOU.
SLOW DOWN, MR. VICE PRESIDENT! THIS IS A RESIDENTIAL DISTRICT!
NO! THIS IS A VICE-RESIDENTIAL DISTRICT!
WE'RE FARMING THOSE BROAD LEDGES --THE VALLEY FLOOR IS PART AGRICULTURAL, PART RECREATIONAL. RESIDENTIAL IS ON THE CLIFFS.
CLAUDE, I'M NOMINATING YOU FOR A HERO OF YLUM AWARD.
GOSH! REALLY?
OZ CANYON
Now Open for Development
Inquire Vice President Claude
VOOPER SIGNS

I ALWAYS KNEW I HAD A DADDY JUST LIKE YOU.
REALLY? I ALWAYS HOPED I'D HAVE DAUGHTERS LIKE YOU AND SCARLET.
BUT IN MY FANTASY, URSULA WAS NOT THE MOTHER.

GO GET THE BIG BOOK, SHEENA, AND I'LL READ YOU A STORY.
OKAY!

HOW I ENVY THE GIRLS. CAN'T YOU SHOW THEIR MOTHER SOME AFFECTION?
YOU TRICKED ME. I HAD A WOMAN I LOVED AND I LOST HER. I'M SORRY --I JUST DON'T FEEL ANYTHING FOR YOU.

I DON'T EVEN KNOW IF I REALLY LOVE THE GIRLS. MY OWN DAUGHTERS. I HOPE SOMEDAY THAT I WILL.
BUT YOU ...?
MAYBE SOMEDAY YOU WILL FEEL SOMETHING FOR ME,TOO.

ANYTHING IS POSSIBLE.

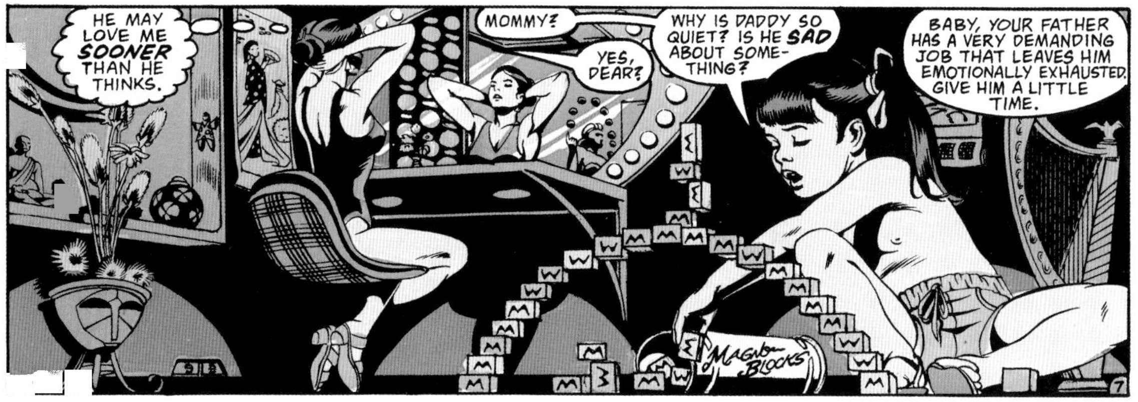

HE MAY LOVE ME SOONER THAN HE THINKS.
MOMMY?
YES, DEAR?
WHY IS DADDY SO QUIET? IS HE SAD ABOUT SOME-THING?
BABY, YOUR FATHER HAS A VERY DEMANDING JOB THAT LEAVES HIM EMOTIONALLY EXHAUSTED. GIVE HIM A LITTLE TIME.
MAGNO BLOCKS
7

WHAT IS DADDY'S JOB?
DADDY IS AN EXECUTIONER, DARLING. HE KILLS THE BAD GUYS.
IS THAT WHY HE KILLED PRESIDENT OGLETHORP?
YES.
I LIKED PRESIDENT OGLETHORP. HE WAS A NICE MAN.

PRESIDENT OGLETHORP WAS STUPID. AND STUPID MEN CAN DO MORE HARM THAN THOSE WHO ARE MERELY EVIL.
CAN I BE AN EXECUTIONER LIKE DADDY?
WE'LL SEE... NOW RUN ALONG. LOOK AFTER YOUR SISTER.

FOR HOURS, NEXUS WANDERS THE NOW DESERTED TUNNELS BENEATH HIS ROOMS.
TUBE-WAYS 3-4-5
EMERGENCY FLARES

UNTIL...

WHERE ARE THE GIRLS?
THEY'RE SLEEPING.

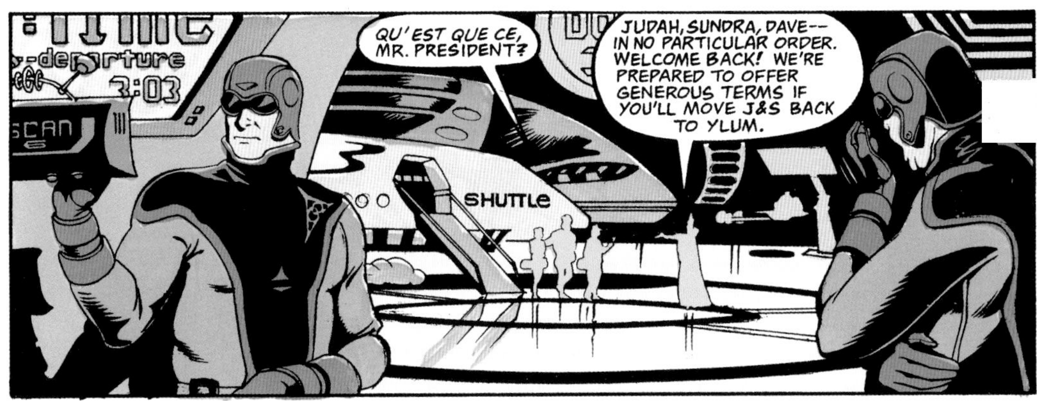
departure
3:03
SCAN
SHUTTLE
QU' EST QUE CE, MR. PRESIDENT?
JUDAH, SUNDRA, DAVE-- IN NO PARTICULAR ORDER. WELCOME BACK! WE'RE PREPARED TO OFFER GENEROUS TERMS IF YOU'LL MOVE J&S BACK TO YLUM.

SORRY, TYRONE. MARS IS WORKING OUT WELL FOR US. ACTUALLY, WE'RE HERE TO BUST NEXUS LOOSE.
YOU KNOW ABOUT KREED.
YES ...
on-air

WE HOPE YOU WON'T OBJECT IF WE TRY TO GET PAST KREED.
I DON'T OBJECT I JUST HOPE YOU DON'T GET HURT.

NO HAY PROBLEMA.
WHAT IT IS!
HEY, BRE'R MEZZ. WOW. LOOK HOW TALL YOU ARE!
YLUM
CHILL YOUR FENDER. WHAT'S THE SKIN ON NEXUS?
THE MAN IS DRIFTING. SHACKED UP WITH THE DRAGON LADY. THE MAN IS STONE CRAZY.

I'LL GET SUNDRA THROUGH THE DOOR, THE REST IS UP TO HER.
IF ANYONE CAN, YOU CAN. BUT YOU'VE GOT TO UNDERSTAND KREED-- HE'S OKAY WHEN YOU GET TO KNOW HIM...
THE DUDE IS LOYAL. AND NEXUS TOLD HIM TO ADMIT NO ONE. HE'LL DIE RATHER THAN STEP ASIDE.

I HOPE IT DOESN'T COME TO THAT.
GATE
9

THE WEE HOURS--AN ARBITRARY DISTINCTION SINCE YLUM DOES NOT HAVE A REGULAR DAY/NIGHT CYCLE.
I ALWAYS WANTED TO FIGHT A QUATRO ASSASSIN, HAR-DE-HAR.
VOUPER WANTS YOU
NEEDED IN

'ROUND ROUND GET AROUND, I GET AROUND ...WHOO-OMMMM..
OH, HI! HOW'S IT GOING?

IT GOES AWAY. NONE MAY ENTER.
DIDN'T YOU DO SOME PRO WRESTLING, UNLIMITED HEAVYWEIGHT? THE SIRIUS CIRCUIT?
NO.

KREED, YOU KNOW ME-- I'M NO LOSER OR BLOB OF DUMB MATTER-- I'M A GOOD FRIEND OF NEXUS.
YOU USED TO BE.
I RESPECT THE HAMMER. BUT NONE MAY ENTER.

WHAT IF IT WERE A MATTER OF LIFE AND DEATH?
THAT'S RIGHT! YOU
IT IS.
KREED, YOU MUST BELIEVE ME. IF WE DON'T GET IN THERE, NEXUS COULD DIE.
I DO NOT BELIEVE YOU. I'VE HEARD IT ALL. FROM EVERYONE.

BELIEVE ME. THERE IS NOTHING YOU CAN DO OR SAY THAT WILL GET YOU THROUGH THAT DOOR. NOT UNTIL GREAT NEXUS WILLS IT.
VERY WELL, YOU'VE MADE YOURSELF CLEAR.

POK
BONK
LONG HAVE I ADMIRED YOUR SKILL, YOUR COURAGE, AND YOUR ELEGANT LANGUAGE.
HA! GOOD FOR YOU, JUDAH! BAD FOR YOU.

THERE IS NO SHAME HERE--YOU DID WHAT YOU HAD TO DO.
I DO WHAT I MUST.
NOK

DO NOT TRY IT AGAIN. I DON'T WANT TO BE REMEMBERED AS THE SLAYER OF JUDAH MACCABEE.

THIS IS CRAZY. THERE'S GOT TO BE A BETTER WAY.
ARE YOU ALL RIGHT?
JUST SOME BRUISES. HUNGH! HE'S TOO GOOD FOR ME TO FIGHT BARE-HANDED.
11

I'LL HAVE TO USE WEAPONS. BETTER HAVE A MEDVAC STANDING BY-- ONE OF US IS GOING TO GET HURT.
WHIRLEY BALLS

GOOD FOR YOU. BAD FOR YOU.
CLICK

THUP THUP THUP THUP THUP THUP THUP

THIP THIP THIP THIP THIP THIP THIP THIP

THUP THUP THUP THUP THUP THUP THUP
KLUD
12

SNAP
THOP
SNAP
STILL LOST
TYRONE RALLY CONCOURS
IT UP!
SLASH
POKE

artifacts ☆☆☆
SPICKLES
STUD SERVICE
ORDER NOW

THUK
14

YAHHHHHHHH

BIF

THUK
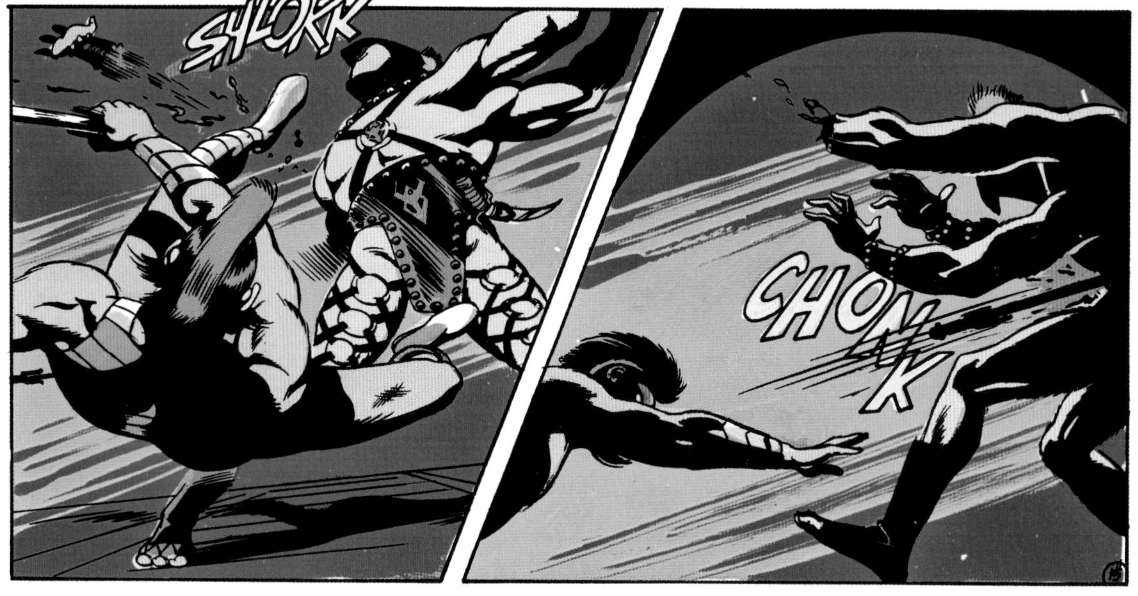
SHLORK
CHONK

COME ON! LET'S GO! STAY AWAY FROM HIM--HE'S STILL DANGEROUS!
OH MY GOD...
STOP-- STOP-- NONE MAY ENTER...

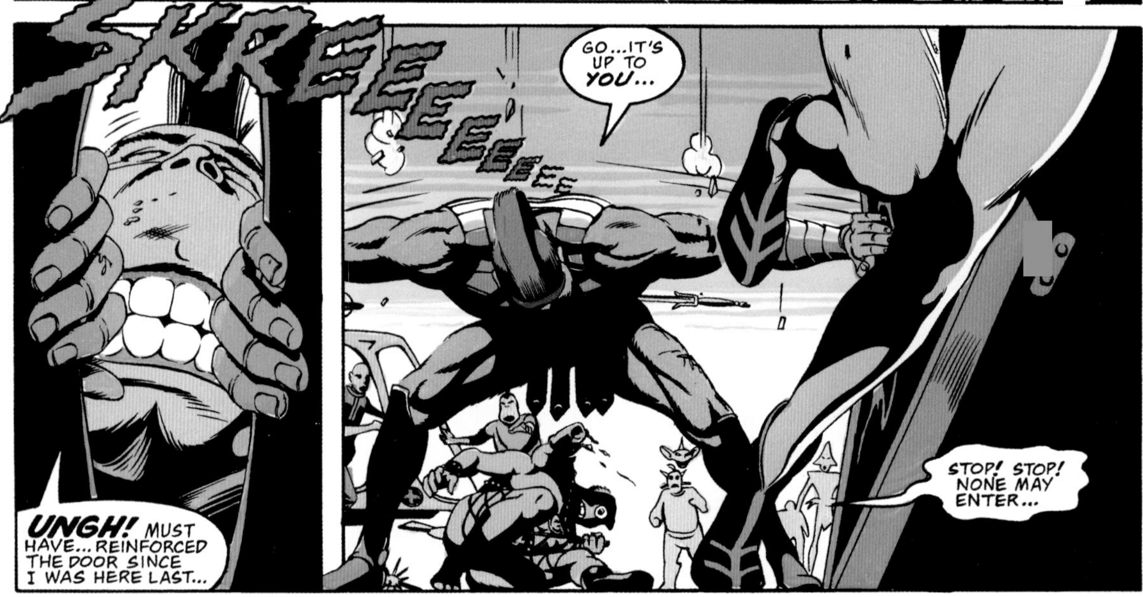
SKREEEEEEEE
GO...IT'S UP TO YOU...
STOP! STOP! NONE MAY ENTER...
UNGH! MUST HAVE...REINFORCED THE DOOR SINCE I WAS HERE LAST...

URSULA!
MOMMY! WHO'S THAT LADY?
The Painted Bird

HOW DARE YOU--!! YOU LEFT HIM! YOU RAN OUT!

16

SCARLETT, TAKE YOUR SISTER AND GO TO YOUR ROOM.

INVESTIGATING A SIMILAR TANK ON HEADWORLD, SUNDRA DISCOVERED WHAT APPEARED TO BE A TRAP DOOR SET FLUSH INTO THE BASE.*
*NEXUS #10
--R.A.O.

THE CURRENT-- INCREDIBLY STRONG--

BUT WHERE AM I GOING?

WHAT?

HORATIO-- SHE'S BACK.
YOOOOOSH!
SUNDRA?

WHERE IS SHE?
SHE WENT DOWN THE DRAIN.
WHAT DRAIN?
IN THE BOTTOM OF THE TANK.

WHERE ARE YOU GOING?
18

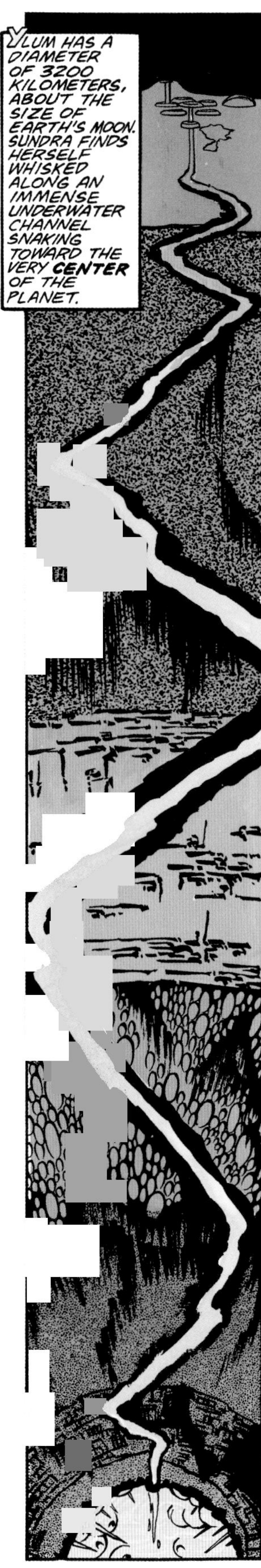
YLUM HAS A DIAMETER OF 3200 KILOMETERS, ABOUT THE SIZE OF EARTH'S MOON. SUNDRA FINDS HERSELF WHISKED ALONG AN IMMENSE UNDERWATER CHANNEL SNAKING TOWARD THE VERY CENTER OF THE PLANET.

MERCIFUL GOD, WHAT HAVE I DONE?

UNTIL AT LAST...
I'M FALLING ...

SPLASH

SO DARK... I SENSE SOME OTHER PRESENCE ...I'LL TURN ON THE LIGHT...
CLICK

19

NEXT MONTH:
THE CREATURE!

TALES from the CLONEZONE™
HALF-CAULKED
I WANT A ROOM. IT MUST BE QUIET. ABSOLUTELY QUIET.
MIKE BARON WORDS
MARK A. NELSON PICTURES
LES DORSCHEID COLORS
STEVE HAYNIE LETTERS
RICK OLIVER DELETIONS
CERTAINLY, MR. FONEBONE, SIR. WE HAVE JUST THE ROOM. FRONT!
THAT'S CLONEZONE.
IF I DON'T GET SOME SLEEP, I'LL BE DEAD-- AND THEN YOU CAN CALL ME WHATEVER YOU LIKE.
RATES
YOU LOOKIN' FOR ACTION, PAL?
NO, I'M LOOKING FOR FOURTEEN HOURS OF UNINTERRUPTED SLEEP.
'CAUSE FEGHOOT'S YOUR MAN. YOU WANT ANYTHING, CALL FEGHOOT.
THAT IS REASSURING. ALL I WANT IS PEACE AND QUIET.
WOMEN, LADY LIZARDS, HOOCH, PILLS, ZAG, YOU NAME IT. FEGHOOT'S YOUR AGENT.
NO THANKS, FEGHOOT-- ALL I WANT IS SLEEP.
HOW ABOUT SOME KNOCK-OUT DROPS? LET YOU SLEEP THROUGH AN EARTHQUAKE.
DON'T NEED IT. NIGHTY-NIGHT, FEGHOOT.

YAWWWWWN
HAIRTOSTE
SWIZZLE
SWIZZLE
ZZZZZZZ
SNORK
BAM
BAM
BAM
BAM
BLINK
BLINK
OPEN UP, FONEBONE! I KNOW YOU'RE IN THERE!
WAIT A SECOND! WAIT A SECOND!
WHERE'S FONEBONE, FLOORLIFE? I'M NOT LEAVING UNTIL I SHOW HIM WHAT HE DID TO MY BASEMENT!
LOOK--I'M NOT FONEBONE. THIS IS MY ROOM. I DON'T KNOW ANY FONEBONE!
UH, WHAT DID HE DO TO YOUR BASEMENT?
WHAT DID HE DO?! I HIRED HIM TO RECAULK MY BASEMENT --A SIMPLE JOB! LOOK! JUST LOOK AT THESE PHOTOS! THREE FEET OF STANDING WATER! THAT'S WHAT HE DID!
I'M NOT LEAVING UNTIL I SEE THE LITTLE RAT!
2

OKAY! OKAY! SEE FOR YOURSELF! GO ON! HAVE A LOOK! THEN MAYBE I CAN GET SOME SLEEP!
YOU BET I WILL, SHORT, GREEN, AND SLIMY!
I AM NOT SLIMY. THAT IS A COMMONLY HELD MISBELIEF--THAT LIZIGATORS ARE SLIMY. WE'RE SMOOTH AND DRY.
I'VE TRAILED FONEBONE ACROSS THE CONTINENT--AND I'LL TRAIL HIM 'CROSS THE GALAXY IF I HAVE TO!
PLEASE... CHECK THE BATHROOM.
OKAY! HE AIN'T HERE! BUT I'VE GOT YOUR NUMBER, LIZARD! I'VE GOT MY EYE ON YOU!
NICE MEETING YOU. YOU MUST CATCH MY ACT SOMETIME.
SLAM
I CAUGHT YOURS.
ZZZZZ
SNORK
ONE HOUR LATER.
CLICK
3

BLINK
CLICK
YAAAAGH!
YIII!!
WHAT ARE YOU DOING IN MY ROOM?
YOUR ROOM?! THIS IS MY ROOM! WHO ARE YOU?
YOU DON'T RECOGNIZE ME? CLONEZONE, IDOL OF MILLIONS? "WHERE THE HELL'S MY COOKIE?"
OH SURE ...THE COMIC.
I'M FONEBONE THE HOME LOAN MAN. GENERAL CONTRACTING, FINANCING TO FIT.
I'VE HEARD OF YOU TOO, FONEBONE. IN FACT...
THERE WAS SOMEONE BY HERE EARLIER LOOKING FOR YOU. SOMETHING ABOUT A LEAKY BASEMENT.
BISMUTH? NOT BISMUTH!!
FELLOW HAD THE SHAPE, SIZE, COLORING, SMELL AND DISPOSITION OF A KODIAK BEAR.
4

BUT IT WASN'T A KODIAK BEAR. I COULD TELL BY HIS DICTION.

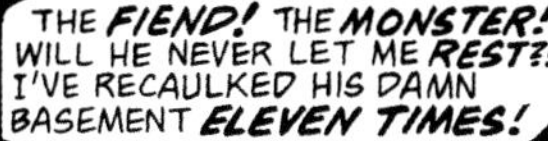
THE FIEND! THE MONSTER! WILL HE NEVER LET ME REST?! I'VE RECAULKED HIS DAMN BASEMENT ELEVEN TIMES!

HE'S HOUNDED ME FROM ONE END OF THE GALAXY TO THE OTHER! I TOLD HIM I COULDN'T GUARANTEE THE JOB! HIS HOUSE IS IN A CAVE ON A MOUNTAINTOP ON CHARON, PLUTO'S ONLY MOON!

Y-Y-YES, I SEE YOUR P-P-POINT...
HE'S A SICK INDIVIDUAL! WHY ELSE WOULD HE LIVE ON CHARON? I TOOK A LOSS ON THE JOB! THE ONLY REASON I EVER AGREED TO IT WAS BECAUSE HE'S MY BROTHER-IN-LAW!
UH-HUH. YOU HAVE MY SYMPATHIES...

BAM! BAM! BAM!
I KNOW YOU'RE IN THERE, FONEBONE!
SMASH
WHAT ABOUT MY BASEMENT, CHISELER?! THREE FEET OF STANDING WATER!

LEAVE ME ALONE! I'LL BUY THE SHULANG PLACE! BUT STOP BUGGING ME ABOUT THAT BASEMENT!
HELLO, DESK? THIS IS CLONEZONE! SEND FEGHOOT!

I DON'T WANT TO SELL THE HOUSE! I WANT A DRY BASEMENT!
I TOLD MY SISTER YOU WERE MESHUGINA!
5

FEGHOOT, I WANT A NEW ROOM! A QUIET ROOM!
FOLLOW ME, SIR.
BUT NO! SHE HAD TO MARRY YOU BECAUSE SHE WAS MESHUGINA!
THIS WAY, SIR. I THINK YOU'LL FIND ALL OUR ROOMS ARE VERY QUIET.
IF YOU NEED ANYTHING...
THANK YOU, FEGHOOT. AND GOODNIGHT!
ZZZZZZ
BAM BAM BAM
YOU'RE A WITNESS TO THIS, LIZARD! FONEBONE JUST PROMISED TO DRAIN THE BASEMENT, RECAULK IT, AND GUARANTEE AGAINST LEAKAGE FOR ONE FULL PLUTO YEAR OR 248 EARTH YEARS--WHICHEVER COMES FIRST!
GET OUT! I'M TRYING TO GET SOME SLEEP!
6

NOBODY SLEEPS UNTIL WE HAVE A DOCUMENT SIGNED AND NOTARIZED!
WHY ME? ALVIN, ALVIN, WHY ME?

BECAUSE YOU'RE A DISINTERESTED THIRD PARTY, THAT'S WHY!
HELLO, FEGHOOT? SEND UP A WORD PROCESSOR, A NOTARY, AND A BOTTLE OF BRANDY.

I DON'T LIKE BRANDY! ORDER SOME TEQUILA!
VERY WELL...

BRING US A BOTTLE OF TEQUILA!
YES SIR!
AND BRING ME A PILL. I'M GOING TO NEED IT.

TELL ME, BISMUTH... WHY DID YOU BUILD ON PLUTO?
IT'S QUIET THERE. I LIKE QUIET.
7

THE NOTARY APPROVES THE CONTRACT.
'S OKAY! PTUI!
SPLAT!

666
WELL GOODNIGHT ...ADIOS ...HASTA LASAGNA...
YOU SHOULD ONLY DEVELOP LUNG CANCER! BOTH OF YOU! I'M SO RATTLED, I HAVE TO TAKE A PILL!
CHARON! BRRRGH! SOUNDS LIKE SHEER HELL.
ZZZZZZZZ
BAM BAM BAM BAM
ZZZ
MR. CLONEZONE...?
DEAD TO THE WORLD. OKAY, GRAB HIS STUFF...
BISMUTH, WE SHOULDN'T BE DOING THIS...
SHADDUP, YOU CRUMMY HOMEWRECKER!
I WANT A DISINTERESTED THIRD PARTY TO SEE YOU DO THE JOB RIGHT THIS TIME!
SO HE GOES TO CHARON WITH US!
END